MAN'S POWER

MAN'S POWER

A Biased Guide to

Political Thought and Action

Kalman H. Silvert

NEW YORK | THE VIKING PRESS

First published in 1970 in a hardbound edition
and a Viking Compass edition by The Viking Press, Inc.
625 Madison Avenue, New York, N.Y. 10022

Published simultaneously in Canada by
The Macmillan Company of Canada Limited

SBN 670-45311-0 (hardbound)
SBN 670-00305-0 (paperbound)

Library of Congress catalog card number: 79-110359

Printed in U.S.A. by The Co onial Press Inc.

To my parents, Henry J. and Ida L., for teaching me
that there can be no love without courage,
and that there is no freedom without love

Contents

Preface

The surface roots of this book were fed by a study I began some nine years ago of the relationship between education and social development in five Latin American cities. A primary hypothesis of that study was that socially mobile persons would be more likely to identify with national community than the occupationally inert. This hypothesis failed in the dozen and a half sample groups studied. This disproof of an important organizing idea led me to speculations about the divisibility of human experiences, which eventually took me to the theoretical views outlined in this book.

The Carnegie Corporation of New York made possible that first study, and with as yet not fully requited patience, permitted me to continue my empirical studies in a follow-up investigation of political and educational attitudes in Chile and Venezuela. This book employs conclusions drawn from the data analysis in these two pieces of research, and can serve as a partial statement of my understanding of those data. Nevertheless, it is an independent work that I hope will stand by itself, and it implies no agreement on the part of my two collaborators in the earlier work—Frank Bonilla in the first study, Leonard Reissman in the second.

Officers of the Carnegie Corporation are also implicated in this work as individuals. I hope that they will accept my gratitude not merely for their material help, but also for actively encouraging me toward making a statement of the modern condition and defending it against the more repressive political aspects of traditionalism.

The tap roots of this little work are buried so deep that I neither know nor want to know where they find their nourishment. Let it be enough to say that I have employed many friends as surrogates for such a profound self-examination, and that they have served me as good and generous people. Teg C. Grondahl, with whom I was formerly associated in the American Universities Field Staff, has taken the manuscript in hand as the master editor that he is. Carl Hamburg, professor of philosophy at Tulane University, brought skill and kindness to bear on a painstaking review of the content and logic of the book. Leonard Reissman, in the sociology department at Tulane, considered the grand lines of the argument and contributed importantly to my summoning up the courage to proceed to publication.

Many of my students in universities in the United States and Latin America have been challenging me to put my pen where for so long I have had my mouth. Their listing would fill many pages. I send them a collective salute and an affectionate embrace, and single out only a few for special mention. First is Morris J. Blachman, my assistant at New York University for three years, and a stubborn and finicky critic of anything he doubts—including portions of this book. John Semack, now at Columbia University, evinces the same qualities of independence of mind combined with an affectionate regard for my feelings. Jerrold Schneider, too, has devoted more time than he could well afford to spare in providing me with comments. Lastly, Joel Jutkowitz, now at San Diego State, can rest content with the knowledge that his long-standing prodding has brought some result.

Laurence Birns seconded Teg Grondahl in turning an editing pen to the manuscript and added his acerbic encouragement. Marlis Krüger provided a touch of the European scrub-brush to my thinking, and S. N. Eisenstadt a sympathetic understanding of what this kind of writing attempts to do.

Needless to say, the only responsibility any of these friends have for the contents of this book is what they choose to assume for themselves.

My secretary at the Ford Foundation, Miss Anna Marie Hein, has been extraordinarily patient and loyal in pushing this book's manuscript through its many versions. In addition, my colleagues there—Reuben Frodin, Lowell Hardin, Nita Manitzas, Raj Rao, Hans Simons, Harry Wilhelm, and others —have helped me bridge the gap between bureaucrat and scholar. They have my gratitude for their exemplary colleagueship.

My wife, senior lecturer in sociology at the City College of New York, has a professional and emotional hand in everything I do. I am overjoyed to be able to say that my oldest son is beginning to be able to do the same. It also touches me to add that even my mother-in-law, Mrs. Dora Moskalik, made valuable suggestions to me concerning content as well as tone. To all these members of my family, as well as to my two younger boys, my gratitude for their demonstration that families can be the scene of intellectual as well as affective and emotional creation.

KALMAN H. SILVERT

Norwich, Vermont
July 30, 1969

Introduction

Political man confounds academic man. "Unpredictable" as-
sassinations change the course of American politics in ways
that scholars are unprepared to define. The greatest military
power on earth, advised by some of its most famous social scientists, cannot find a way to win a "bush" war without undertaking its own national mobilization or literally erasing the
enemy. Urban violence was not a subject high on the social-
science priority list in the decade before the outbreak of black
rebellions in American cities.

Social danger lurks in the pit between the capacity of political theory to explain and the increasing number and
velocity of events that need to be understood. Explanations,
however, are unavoidable, even though they may be the
wrong ones. If we are unable to develop guides to understanding that are at least partially validated by events, then
we shall simply be making do with magical explanations. We
shall continue to use great-man theories to explain French or
American politics. We shall go on thinking that such men as
Castro and Ho Chi Minh and their followers are "crazy"
because they are willing to incur massive sanctions by flout-

ing American foreign policy. We shall have nothing saner to offer the public in place of its prevailing paranoid conspiracy theories about international events and internal disorder. Theories based on the premise of man's inherent stupidity and evil are simple to use, because they are undemonstrable; to enunciate them is to prove them. But the peril is that they create social reality. Strong men act on them, and weak men follow. Ritualistic acceptances of the "obvious" lace into the design of foreign-aid programs, armies are mobilized and used in accordance with them, citizens both conservative and liberal vote by their lights, and our children inherit a world of quicksand. Bad ideas produce bad politics—a politics that inhibits rational predictions and is thus inherently unstable, a politics whose predictions can be made to come "true" only by using overt force.

Of course, there are political theories available that can, in matter-of-fact ways and without fibrous terminology, help us understand contemporary political happenings. But there are also a great many irrelevant political theories in common currency. In fact, it is probably the irrelevant ones that reign today in the social sciences, if we judge on the basis of which ones are favored by those who profess to explain grand politics in most university classrooms and public forums. Many of the most widely used contemporary theory books do not have such words as "power" and "social class" and "values" and "ideology" in their indexes. Their authors, trying to explain universal political phenomena, ignore those common and indispensable words which have meaning only in specific historical circumstances. This desire for global breadth is praiseworthy, but the search for "general theory" as expressed today is unlikely to succeed, because it does not include a concomitant search for the ways in which particular situations can be related to general ones. Scholars in the university are reasonably well equipped to talk in a general way about what is the same in Germany as, let us say, a Makonde village, but we are hard put to explain the reasons for the precise differences between Swedish and German political history. If the university is to be useful to the polity, this flaw is most serious, for it inhibits the application of theory to any particular set of social facts. A truly general theory would explain at least a significant number of the relations possible among individuals, social groups, and total societies—as well as the likenesses and differences across all societies through all time.

Whatever the present state of social theory, I do not think I am exaggerating the gap between it and political action. Much has been made recently of the disaffection in the United States between the intellectual and the government. Indubitably, personality and policy have conditioned this estrangement. But there are also some institutional facts of life that have spawned animosity. Many public officials feel that the advice they receive from social scientists is impractical, unrealistic, beside the point, "soft-headed." For their part, many social scientists believe that the government is in the hands of know-nothings, supported by an equally ignorant populace force-fed on the delicacies of television and on the other pap of our multi-media civilization. At the same time, a cadre of "hard-nosed" social scientists has worked closely with administrations prepared to show them hospitality. At this moment I am not concerned with the ideology of these attachments or disaffections, but rather with the formal institutional relations they imply, and the correlation between them and what the academic community is providing our government.

The modern university has its organizational roots in late medieval times. Modern science as an organized undertaking dates only from the seventeenth century. The ideal university format and its scientific and humanistic functions as they have developed since then are an exquisite harmony of form and substance. The university's autonomy was meant to separate the institution from immediate social pressures so that it could permit and protect freedom of thought and experimentation. The exercise of academic freedom within that institutional frame is what the professor accepts as his primary charge. He bears that responsibility in payment for the tenure which is his personal token of the autonomy's practical significance. Societies at large permit some of their members the luxury of such freedom with limited sanction because of the expected social pay-off: the fruits of their competence. The surest way to academic incompetence (and thus irrelevance) is by destroying university autonomy and academic freedom. Still, violations of its autonomy by forces outside the university are all too common. Book censorship, military invasions of classrooms, legislative injunctions concerning text materials and curricula, and sometimes the effects of "student power" movements are ordinary fare in the daily press. Not so publicized are the surrenders of academic freedom by academic men who assume political positions that endanger their ability to carry out responsibly free research in the future or, even worse, inhibit their ability to teach students freely for fear of making them privy to information stamped "confidential."

The freedom necessary for the day-to-day work of physical and natural scientists is easily given in modern states. After all, how many people pretend to understand physics anyway? However, if for reasons of political conviction the physicist steps out of his laboratory to argue against, say, the making of particular weapons, then he may be found to be a "security risk" and denied the freedom he once enjoyed in his work. If he similarly exceeds the bounds of his professional competence by lecturing on the politics of winning guerrilla wars, however, he may be honored by a political establishment that likes to bolster its policy claims with the prestige of his support. Since social-science competence is difficult to come by, difficult to recognize, and even more difficult to employ unideologically, the "hard" scientist is welcomed as a political expert.

It is difficult to accord to studies of society the same institutional guarantees given to the intellectual endeavors that are protectively wrapped in the mists of aesthetics or the mysteries of the laboratory. In a society dedicated to the notion that everybody can be his own political scientist, special privileges, or the weight of prestige, are extended only doubtfully to the professional engaged in that academic discipline. This dubiety is only reinforced when the social scientist himself rushes to become a practitioner—often while still pretending to academic autonomy and freedom. He asks his students, his colleagues, and his society to presume his saintly objectivity; he asks his government to presume both his acceptance of its nonacademic goals and his enduring competence in the absence of continued validation of his premises. This arrogance often goes rewarded.

The first condition of a useful political science is that it permit significant diagnosis and verifiable prediction, both based on procedures open to replication. A dangerous political science, by my criteria, is one whose formulators try to apply their learning to the making of policy in the government—as distinct from persons who make professional and technical advice available without themselves attempting to suggest or set policy. In short, I automatically trust the political instincts of my colleagues no more than anybody else's.

In saying this, I dissociate myself from the ranks of the Platonists and from their philosopher-king argument, and align myself with those who propose that a good political system is one that keeps personal idiosyncrasy where it belongs— far away from dictating to others how to live their lives.

I have expressed this bias because I intend to turn it into a stricture on myself in this book. I would like to close the gaps between the policy-makers and citizens and myself—not by telling political leaders what they should do but, rather, by advancing a schema in the hope that it might help us all to understand better what our choices may be. As a citizen, I certainly reserve the right to make what noise I can, and will; but as a social scientist, I must recognize that my opinions as a citizen are rooted in the fertile mud of personality, just like anyone else's.

Naturally I hope to help those who share my ideological bias to be more effective in politics than we have been in the past. Because any scientific bias is necessarily rationalistic and because my personal ideology is unabashedly rationalistic, I presume that perhaps only rationalists will care to read this book or that only they among my readers will know why they accept or reject it. But there are many citizens who accept an essentially pragmatic, relativistic, and evidential approach to politics. While I am sure some of them will reject my approach, I trust that they will share with me the essential notion that libertarianism and rationalism are political correlates. Accept that as a starting point, and I can address this book to rationalists of the democratic left *and* right.

Although my political head tells me to search for this broad spectrum of readership, my political heart tells me that I am really writing for libertarian rebels. I should be profoundly pleased if I could say something useful or meaningful to the new generation of university students, from Berkeley to Prague, from New York and Buenos Aires; to black power leaders, urban reformers, and seekers of freedom and dignity in the developing countries; to persons at all social levels and in all walks of life who sympathize with those people's aspirations for a decent life. Conversely, I wish ill to totalitarians, prophets of needless cruelty and violence, and all those who take power into their hands for their own sententiously prideful benefit, "natural" rulers because they have seized power whose use they are often shameless enough to justify as being God-given.

Still, I may have already lost many of those whom I would like to address, not least because I use forbidden words. I have written, for example, the word "democratic." To the shame of the developed countries, that term is now regarded as a synonym for corruption and inefficacy by most of the politicized groups in the developing countries. For the left, democracy is a cover for imperialism; for the right, it is part of their international alliance system for the containment of domestic dissidence. In addition, I have praised "rationalism," when romanticism is a necessity for many movements championing change. I have also denounced "prophets of needless cruelty and violence" at a time when Algerians and Cubans and many black nationalists are convinced that without the cleansing experience of violence, the shattered souls of the miserable cannot be made whole.

A viable political theory for today must take into account some of these and other current objections to a libertarian approach. The debates concerning the tensions between order and freedom, individual and society, and authority and liberty have a long and complex history. English and American natural law doctrine prescribes when a citizen should declare his government illegitimate. "Democracy for whom" is a thorny issue of power distribution coming to us in a straight line from Magna Carta to Gideon. The Encyclopedists, the existentialists, and the technocrats were and are still in an uncompleted debate concerning what we are to be rationalistic about, and what should command our romantic, unreasoning acceptance. No one can provide definitive answers to these and the other political problems I shall explore; what I should like is to present a coherent pattern of the ingredients and patterns of political behavior, so that the reader may be better equipped to do whatever he wishes with those postulations.

I am not sure where and when and from whom I learned and managed a certain integration of many of the ideas that inform the following discussion. I like to tell myself that a long line of secularist and rationalist thinkers provided me with the core of my understanding—from Machiavelli to Locke and Adam Smith, from the British utilitarians and Kant to Weber and Cassirer in this century, by way of Marx. All these men teach us to think of the social environment as the product of human ordering. They also suggest that the prime ethical purpose of order, and its only long-term assurance, is the furthering of individual autonomy. Of course, other themes can be drawn from all of them, especially from Machiavelli and Marx. But my use of these and other thinkers in this book is frankly exploitative: I take from them what they suggest to me, without any attempt to re-create their thinking or even to quote from them.

Conversely, there are other theorists I reject. For the purpose of this discussion, I have little use for Hegel and the Romantics, as well as that part of Marx which remains in that tradition. Hobbes and his cult bore me, and the French

Rationalists are too coy for my taste. Still, they have plainly influenced my thinking, and so have many of my contemporaries.

I make no claim to originality in my identification of significant parts of society or theories of social ethics, but I hope the ordering of those elements is fresh and useful. My purpose is to write about politics in a contained, old-fashioned, quasi-polemical way; my own ethical views, however, demand that what I say be subject to disproof or verification by research into the actualities of political behavior. Therefore, I do not ask the reader to accept my premises, but only to judge whether they are useful for political analysis and action.

In writing a speculative essay of this kind, it seems to me, one reaches a certain height of immodesty, for one presumes this his unsupported views are worth the reader's time. To write this book I have put aside my scruples in this respect—not for academic but for political reasons. I want to persuade others that when democratic society gets into trouble, it is not because there is too much freedom, but because there is too little. My own life, I am selfish enough to believe, may well depend on a reasoned acceptance of this idea, which I see as more than a light bit of social truth. And I think that many other lives also depend on a widespread belief in tenable democratic ideas—including the lives of the present enemies of public decency.

Theses

The task of this book is to explore the relation between constraints and freedoms in the human political condition. This statement does not easily lend itself to a testable social theory. It raises the old questions of free will and determinism, of the nature of man and his works; and it raises rather newer questions about the individual and the class order, ideology and communications systems, and the tensions between order and freedom in industrial society.

The time has passed in which moral pleading could pass for political theory. Moral pleas can still be politically effective and sometimes intellectually pleasing, but rarely can they serve as guides to scholarly work. Most academic investigation, on the other hand, is intra-systemic and does not put entire situations into question, which the moralist must always do. The methodological purpose of this book is to build a testable social theory that is also an overtly ideological one. In consequence of this design, the methodological purpose is the same as the theoretical and ideological ones: I seek to show that there are reasonable grounds for assuming that an explanatory theory also reveals something about political man that is an ethical good worth pursuing in its own right.

The theses of this book, in their baldest terms, are as follows:

—The explanation of social causation requires consideration of the role played by human decision and the range of its play.

—The essential measure of political development is the relation between the range of choice open to a polity and the range it actually explores.

—The essential measure of political modernization is the degree to which ritualistic decisions to act cede to rational determinations in political choice-making.

—The regularities we study should include not only the ways polities maintain themselves, but also the ways in which system-breaking leaps are made. The latter most clearly show the need for an ordered (and ordering) theory of the interplay between constraint and effectiveness of choice.

—Making effective choices that permit wider arrays of choices to be made in the future is a good in itself.

—"Good" politics, a politics that widens the areas of effective choice, is desirable in itself, a public interest whose defense is worth while intrinsically as well as because it is essentially identical with private interest.

MAN'S POWER

■ Elements of Politics

Concerning certain schools of social explanation;
the importance of values, class, institutions,
and personal temperament; the definition
of these factors; and a plea for forbearance

Let us begin by taking inventory of the stock. The purpose of this chapter is to explore the structures of the major components of political life. I ask the reader to refrain from connecting these components for the time being. Such forbearance will be difficult, for most systems of political thought consider these components to be either lineally linked or chaotically disordered. That is, given one set of social facts, such as feelings of economic deprivation, some theories posit a series of necessary reactions that cause a certain kind of predetermined political behavior. Others maintain that there is no such neat patterning of human events, that the deity, accidents of personality, or chance are what truly determine our situation. Both types of theories are aesthetically and scientifically unsatisfying, and politically depressing. They imply that man has neither the privilege nor the power to choose among various courses of action: that built-in psychological or other motor forces keep him functioning on a self-adjusting course (equilibrium theories), or drive him inevitably toward perfection (Marxist theories), or push him upward to God (Hegelian theories). As for the deistic theories, they hold that man and his action are shaped by a "will" outside the human experience (St. Thomas) or, at best, by the wills of super-humans (Carlyle).

Religious or casual theories of politics by definition are immune to rational analysis and can be argued only by tenuous analogies, if at all. The bias of this book therefore precludes their being taken with intellectual seriousness, though they can understandably be taken with the fervor of dogma. And, indeed, most men seem to prefer this-worldly rather than other-worldly explanations, at least when they can get them. Even Einstein could not abide the thought that physical change might be as another toss of the dice, unless even the latter was empirically determinable. The need to understand life as something more than a game of probabilities is too easily satisfied by lineal and single-cause explanations. However tempting, these explanations also lure us into confusing the general with the specific. The leap from universal principle to specific social practice without intermediate explanatory theory has, as a rule, proved intellectually and politically disastrous.

We may laugh at the primitive belief that devouring the heart of a brave man will make the eater as courageous as the eaten. But is it such a far cry from that to the geopolitician's premise that physical location and circumstance determine the nature of society? Racial determinism, vulgar economic determinism, the idea that value systems determine social action, and all other simplistic causal views also lead inevitably to miscalculations in domestic and foreign politics. To be sure, diet, climate, natural resources, physical attributes, religious and other ethical systems, and economic and other institutional organization have much to do with politics. But it is incorrect to assume that any one of them can be singled out as ordaining the course of human action. Rather, each one places limits—sometimes extremely loose ones—upon behavior. Social behavior, moreover, is only grossly circumscribed by even rather strict limits. To take an elementary example, clearly a country with no coal and iron within its borders will not have coal and iron mines, yet it may well have a steel industry if other factors make it possible to import the necessary raw materials. Or, to take a more complex example, a country with a far-flung industrial establishment would, given today's technology, also reveal urbanization and an elaborate communications system, but these attributes will not necessarily coexist with an equitable distribution of income, a democratic political system, or egalitarian public education.

The biological sciences, enjoying innovative breakthroughs, are beginning to feed new unilineal explanations into the stock of political theory, with interpretations of the behavior of all living creatures on a single continuum, in which at least part of what we have been calling human nature is seen as merely a part of more general animal behavior. For example, hierarchy, territoriality, and the survival value of aggressiveness are phenomena that can be widely observed in the animal world; and they are concepts that, by analogy, tell us something about human behavior. There is some mild social usefulness in knowing that certain goldfish swim in a kind of power hierarchy, that animals stake out their territories according to various devices or stratagems, and that knowing when to fight and when to run has something to do with staying alive long enough to have offspring. It is comforting to know that epicanthic folds are useful in protecting the eyes from cold and that pigmentation inhibits sunburn. It is more socially useful, however, to know that goggles also can protect eyes and that suntan lotions have been invented to protect the skin. To mention these examples is but another way of saying that universal phenomena have a distant, attenuated social meaning, and their discovery is largely an empirical, descriptive matter.

Of true significance for social thinking, and much more difficult to arrive at, are not the biological or geographical frontiers that define our being at any given historical moment, but rather the ways in which individuals and societies have chosen their variations on the common themes of humanity. Ordering this variability is an empirical task, surely, but it is also a theoretical one. Our scholarly and commonsense obligation is to discriminate between occurrences which are naturally bound together and those which are related because man himself, in his many cultures, has wittingly or unwittingly bound them. This discrimination between the *naturally* and so *necessarily* tied, and the *culturally* and so *temporally* tied, is the first step in making reasoned choices. Why labor fruitlessly on what cannot be helped? Why surrender will in areas that can respond to human decisions?

During this century social scientists have taken an important tack in their attempt to describe all human organization through all times and culture systems—the analogue of the search for biological or geographical constants. The major school of such "general theorists" is usually called "functionalist," because it has found that comparable social functions can be isolated everywhere, even though the institutional ordering of such functions is historically specific. For example, throughout all social time, mankind has produced children, a functional requisite for system-maintenance. Societies institutionalize this functional requisite by socializing their children, rationalizing their surroundings,

seeking predictability for them as they grow, building co-
ercive mechanisms, adjudicating their disputes, allocating
resources, and so on. As man cannot escape environmental
imperatives, though he can change their definition by
applied invention; and as he cannot escape biological imperatives, though he may delay them or silt them over culturally—so he cannot escape the functional demands of
human society, though he may carry them out well or badly,
in sacred or secular belief-systems, or in a wide variety of
institutional arrangements. Thus, the functionalist school of
political analysis seeks to "separate out analytically the structures which perform political functions in all societies regard-
less of scale, degree of differentiation, and culture." [1]

In this discussion, I have moved from single-cause and
lineal theories to geographical, biological, and functional
attempts to frame the whole of human experience. The common denominator of all these constructions is that they
attempt a total explanation from an intellectual base somewhere outside of man's historical experience. Now I see
nothing objectionable in aspiring to a universal theory of
social action, but to argue that there is a master principle, or
even a set of principles, to which societies conform is not the
way to achieve it. As I have suggested in the preface, these
approaches do not provide sufficient conditions for explaining any particular set of historical facts; they collapse when
we apply them to particular cases. Further, the ideological
effect of such views is to persuade us that the ways in which
man can make his own world are depressingly limited. Even
though it can logically be denied that this implication necessarily flows from such teachings as those of the functionalist

[1] Gabriel A. Almond and James S. Coleman, *The Politics of the Developing Areas* (Princeton, N.J.: Princeton University Press, 1960), p. 5.

school, its proponents find it hard to respond when they are pressed to explain the range of man's past variability and the possibilities for his future variability. *As an empirical matter,* within the limitations imposed by science, technology, and general understanding, to what extent can man truly create himself and his world? *As a projective matter,* removing the constraints of given bodies of scientific, technological, and other knowledge, to what extent can man truly create himself and his world? *As an academic matter,* what kind of theory is required to analyze data so as to answer these questions? Certainly theories that do not permit historical analysis (and thus an ordered knowledge of cultural particularity) cannot reveal the connections between limiting, or guiding, principles on the one hand, and the specific creations of which man has been and, we hope, will be capable on the other.

By no means should we discard the insights provided by the various approaches to general theory. What I propose is to downgrade them in the hierarchy of theory on the grounds that the significant and relevant questions of politics and society in general arise from the study of generalizable particularities, not universals. We know that all men must take nourishment, discharge certain roles bearing certain statuses, go through a socialization process, and so forth. The societal significance of these constants is made manifest only when we put order into the questions of *what* men eat, *which* roles have what kind of status position in given conditions, and *how* socialization patterns spread within and among societies. Then, when we proceed to relate socialization processes to the distribution of status and then to consumption patterns, we are in a position to learn when and how we can transfer explanations from one social situation to another. We have to think simultaneously of the universal and the unique, the generalizable and the particular, the variable and the invariable. Thus, instead of seeing general theory as the highest order of speculative thought, we might well consider it the lowest, concerning as it does the immutable foundation on which social beings build variation. The more complex and difficult level of theorizing is, surely, the one that tries to discover the causes of variation, rather than identify the invariable.

Both substantive and procedural consequences flow from the attempt to marry theories of universal generality to those of historical uniqueness. A basic practical result is that we can measure the effects of universals on a single scale, which, like a ruler, measures in the same units along its entire length. When we are dealing with historical happenings, however, any such continuum as a ruler or a scale is useless for measuring differing qualities. In order to discipline the uniqueness of historical events, we must employ typologies— sets of categories linked by the wit of the observer for the purpose of showing how differing happenings relate to one another, whether in harmony or dissonance. Our natural tendency when we construct continua is to presume that change flows smoothly from one point on the scale to another. When we deal with groupings of unique events we may also submit to the temptation to see change as proceeding evenly within each category, but in addition we tend to forewarn ourselves to the possibility of disruption and disturbance when social situations change from one family of events to another. Each method thus threatens us with a trap in interpreting substance: invariables need unchanging measures that emphasize continuity and order; variables need an assortment of measures that highlight breaks in process and disorder.

An additional consequence shows itself in research design. For scholars interested in specific cases, universals assume theoretical significance only insofar as they impose limits on the interplay of the variables in each case under study. The social ethic of this point of view is that whatever is universal can be assumed to be value-neutral, but the governing question for moral judgment (as well as for research) is not what constraints do to man, but rather what man does with his constraints. Here is one of those rare places in which the intertwining of ideological and scientific commitment is entirely clear, for it is both an ethical and a theoretical commitment to assume that research will be better served if functional universals are treated as limiting and descriptive, but not as controlling.

I shall return to these questions, but here the principal purpose of putting this argument has been to persuade the reader that there is sufficient doubt about the processes of social change to justify my earlier request that for the time being he suspend any inclination to think of elements of politics as connected in a particular way.

The elements of politics: if we want to diagnose and predict the behavior of political man and political men, then I think we need to begin by learning the following about them:

—Their value-systems. Here I include people's basic worldviews: their norms, religious beliefs, their most profound biases and prejudices. In other words, we need to know the value-significance with which men imbue the facts of social situations.

—The potential power or effectiveness of individuals in groups: not their *specifically* political power, but, rather, the advantages with which they were born (their life-chances, to use Weber's term), their potential ability to control goods and men on the economic marketplace, their power to command deference and prestige and to manipulate other institutional levers *if they so desire*. We need to know the situations of individuals within the stratification or class system of their society.

—Their institutional locations: the types of relations individuals and groups have to social institutions; also the patterns of institutional orders, their real and ideal interlocking. Included are the "big five" institutions—family, religion, economy, education, and polity—and also such ancillary structures as political parties, pressure groups, trade unions, ladies' auxiliaries of veterans' organizations, and so forth.

— The actors' personal characteristics. Is Senator so-and-so lazy and stupid and covered with the patina of an Ivy League education? Or is he active and intelligent and the product of a cow college? Is our subject even-tempered, or irascible, possibly paranoid? When we think about groups, what personality types are idealized and liable to political success within them? What are the recipes for personal success in a Junior Chamber of Commerce, a legislature, a union, a rural school district?

These elements are listed in the order in which I think them susceptible to change. The subject will be explored later, but at this point it is worth denying any special significance to the requirement of language and thought that they appear somehow in a given order. For present purposes the order might as well have been reversed, and a detailed explanation of the elements will indeed employ another order.

The list omits specific mention of functions, of course, and it merely implies issues of status and role. For reasons I have given, the emphasis is on searching for the range of social variation, and universal imperatives will therefore have to stand aside. The kind of paradigm I am looking for should have special relevance to problems of politics, and should differentiate among historical manifestations of all political occurrences. The elements of the system should thus have universal presence but should also be susceptible to differentiation by empirical means. In addition, they should be directly relevant to the creation and aggregation of public power or political efficacy; and they should be useful for cross-cultural as well as single-country political analysis. They ought also to be theoretically independent of one another, so that their juxtaposing and contraposing permit the construction of many models, reflecting many social relations. Last, these elements should suggest other levels of generalization and should be easily usable in research and politics.

Whether these four principal elements of political behavior answer to these criteria is part of the burden of proof which falls on the remainder of the discussion. So let us examine each in some detail, starting this time with the power measure, since it is the one most immediately significant for politics.

Social Stratification

This element most easily fulfills the criteria of acceptability I have just advanced. Talcott Parsons has summarized the centrality of the concept as follows: "It has come to be widely recognized . . . that social stratification is a generalized aspect of the structure of all social systems, and that the system of stratification is intimately linked to the level and type of integration of the system as a whole." [2] That is, social stratification is universal, but the way of stratification is particular and tells us much about the nature of each kind of system. Social differentiation by sex and age is everywhere with us, for example, and even these elementary distinguishing marks among people have political consequences so obvious that I will not reach for examples.

But stratification pure and simple is not enough if we are trying to see how to detail the differences between highly complex and primitively structured societies. In the latter, we can expect to find that all children will be born with roughly the same societal chances for success. Survival in itself may well be the key to becoming a political leader in many Mayan villages, for example. More important for our purposes are stratification systems that reveal wide differences in life style from stratum to stratum, carrying across generations and defining the caste or class systems. In the standard definitions, caste systems are rigid in the sense that mobility across the dividing lines is virtually impossible, while class systems presume some kind of permeability, or staining, from one segment of the system to another.

How are these divisions—stratification, caste, and class—useful in political analysis? Any stratification system can be used to define a system of power distribution, baldly considered. That is, the difference between men and women, for example, as it reveals itself in what each does in given societies, implies a difference in power. Women may have

[2] *Essays in Sociological Theory*, rev. ed. (Glencoe, Ill.: The Free Press, 1954), p. 386.

more power than men in socializing children, less in the politics of inter-tribal and intra-tribal relations, more in economics if they look after the crops and decide on consumption allocations. Caste systems, since they reinforce occupational differences, also underscore religious, political-power, and many other differences. But the most subtle manifestations of power and stratification show up in *class* analysis. Indeed, the subtlety is sometimes so great that in countries such as the United States many will deny that classes exist at all, perhaps because of the prevailing mythology that we are all truly equal before society's engines. In this situation, of necessity, class as a simple power measure cannot exist, and everyone contentedly calls himself part of the middle class—except those so powerless they cannot fool even themselves into believing that they are participating members of the national structure.

To me, the Weberian definition of social class is the most satisfying as a starting point, although I have reservations about it. Weber argued that the social structural position of groups is defined by their "class" or economic position, their "status" or prestige position, and their "party" or political position. He further presumed that the economic measure was the primary one, that through time it determined the status and political measures. I should like to amend this approach in three ways. In the first place, I should like to change the nomenclature, speaking instead of economic power, social power, and political power. In the second place, I should like to argue that in short and intermediate terms (the time spans that most interest us for political purposes) changes in one or another of the hierarchies can occur in relative independence of the others, and certainly can occur without the economic one having to come first. (This presumption needs elaboration, for it cuts across the grain of much conventional wisdom as well as some standard theory.) Third, *I should like to use class to refer to power only in the sense of its potential use.* That is, all other things (values, institutions, personal characteristics) being equal, what can given classes and persons within them do if they want to? We have to put to one side the *facts* of how society operates if we divide class power from the institutions through which most of that power is made manifest or is generated. Nevertheless, it helps us to think about the matter if we separate a reservoir of power (class) from the spillways (institutions) through which it passes. And, admittedly, it is confusing to think of class as a pool of potential power only, when such power resists measurement until it is put to use. It is easier to discover who does what to whom than to discover who *might* do what to whom. Disentangling class from institutional orders is also operationally confusing, because if we define class as a conglomerate of abilities flowing from and to economic and political institutions and reinforced by a normative acceptance called status, we may end by reducing class, institutions, and values to an indistinguishable blur. Still, the necessity for differentiating between class and institution is clear. Not the least of the advantages arising from the separation is that it enables us to trace power through generations, and thus to see how class affects behavior patterns and personal values. One of the more interesting subjects in politics is the mapping of the recruitment pools from which the leaders and their followers come. How much movement is there among these pools from generation to generation? How do cultural styles and modes of acceptance either strengthen or threaten their continuance?

In sum, then, we are obliged to use institutional and normative data from which to derive class descriptions. In this view, class must be analyzed through social time; it is an intergenerational measure, established by charting power *application* toward the end of projecting power *potential*. The fundamental differences between class and institutionalized behavior are thus matters of time and effect, distinguishable by using the same indicators differently. Institutional statuses and roles tell us who can do what to whom today. Class tells us who is likely to do what to whom in the future, while it also informs us about the dynamics of how leader-subject positions were filled in the past.

The clinching example that shows why we must think of class and institutions as separate derivatives of the same measures is the fact of revolution. When existing institutions undergo rapid, drastic change, we have revolution; if a shift in relative class power occurs through revolutionary action (if the order of probabilities of recruitment changes, in other words), it is the result of the generation and accumulation of power by groups perhaps previously denied the routine satisfaction of their aspirations. For instance, an institutional order may well need a literate lower class but attempt to deny it political participation. That kind of lower class can create further power by means of organization (itself an institutional phenomenon) and can then work the institutional upheaval we call revolution. If we think of power applied only overtly and immediately, we could not talk of this "generator-storage battery" phenomenon.

The operational difficulty of defining social class is compounded when we assume—as we have done—a certain independence among the measures of potential power. Let us take a very simple example from the elementary European history taught to all of us. We learned that in feudal society he who had economic power also had social and political power; to know one was to know the others. It was explained that the re-emergence of city-states in northern Italy, the Low Countries, and a few other places created a group of artisans—persons with new economic power. Slowly, as the nation-state form (if not its full social organizational content) emerged, the economic middles began to clamor for political rights and social acceptance, which eventuated in the archetypal French Revolution. Whatever the complexities of social change during that period, the "natural" way to think of it was as moving from the economic to the political. But evidence drawn from presently modernizing societies offers clear proof that what may well have been the distinctive mark of the class coherence of medieval society and the patterns of its undoing does not now hold, for in these societies, to know the economic situation of a group is not necessarily to know its status or political power, even through fairly long time periods. For example, some of the wealthiest persons in Chile are Lebanese mill owners, who have dominated textile manufactures in that country for almost a century. Despite their great wealth, until very recently they were denied access to the status approval of the aristocracy and even suffered "negative" political power in the form of harassment, special taxation, and the like. In this unevenness of their power potential, of course, they resemble Jews and other pariah peoples in many countries.

What can be easily demonstrated with regard to ethnically and religiously identifiable snub-groups is also not difficult to show for other groups not so marked. Latin America's rural middle class is comprised of tailors, schoolteachers, low-level farm administrators, and others of this nature who have small monetary incomes, local but practically no national political power, and a status considerably above that possessed by the Indian or laboring mestizo populations. On any national scale these people fall into the lower-class economic and political position, while on the scale of status they are on a kind of lower middle-class level, the fruit of their being of European culture. A usual way for them or their children to rise in power is on the social-status or the political ladder. The climb up the social ladder starts when such persons send their children to a national or provincial university, whether or not the student is eventually graduated; the political ladder also often leads through an educational institution, in particular the military academy. So a rather standard life-history of a member of a Latin American "new elite" starts with a modest rural birth, proceeding to local primary schooling, a military academy, a rapid castrensic career, entry and ascent in politics, and then economic success. Thus the person goes from a curve that is low in economic power, middle in social power, and low in political power, to one that is high in economic power, up but a little in social power, and high in political power. (His children will have the opportunity to even out their prestige positions, which they, too, begin by acquiring appropriate educational certification.)

Most Latin American countries gained their independence early in the nineteenth century, but the new states of Africa and Asia are recently enough arrived so that we do not have to stretch our memories when we subject their quasi-revolutionary experiences to this kind of class analysis. In the Gold Coast, for example, the British Colonial Office acted as the upper class: political power and high status were theirs; and national economic power centered in British companies involving cacao and a few other commodities welcomed on the international market. A few natives had what might be called an upper-middle economic position. Kwame Nkrumah and his followers supplanted the British rulers as the effective upper class by a change in their own class position that opened up the kingdom of politics. Economic power was overthrown by political power.

These examples are all familiar enough. I advance them merely to repeat several theoretical points: in the short run, political power can be created in ways independent of economic determinations; to think of class as potential power has the added utility of relating the dynamics of domestic to international politics, where the naked play of power is persistently clear; and, last, the concept of class employed in this fashion is as useful for explaining the behavior of large groups as it is for charting the mobility moves of individuals.

These primitive beginnings of political thought are often denied in word and practice. To hold that "money talks" is a common rebuttal. After World War II when Communist parties in developing lands argued that they had to create a bourgeoisie in order subsequently to destroy it, they were following a line which the actions of Castro later clearly denied. Castro also proved that an island seemingly buried under American economic power could literally brave fire, flood, and storm in political action that defied Cuba's faltering economy.

The domestic scene in the United States is also not immune to this kind of analysis. C. Wright Mills' power-elite argument is one testimony to the possibilities of class analysis. The work of the "community power" opponents of his monolithic analysis does not deny in itself the validity of a class approach. Their counterargument merely is that the destiny of the nation is not in the hands of an interlocking directorate of political-economic-military groups and their satellite celebrities, as Mills says, because power is divided and subdivided and otherwise scrubbed about at state and local levels. That may be so, but another possibility is that national leaders in all important posts across the board tend to be chosen, or to offer themselves, from a broad but still circumscribed class group or, more likely, complex of class groups, which only rarely includes any of the deprived social categories. We may also find that national leaders are recruited from a somewhat different class segment than local leaders. If so, we might well expect them to clash on such issues as race, schooling, "order in the streets," taxation, and so forth, and that the voices of the underprivileged will be heard only indirectly. Could such antagonisms be an American variant on the theme of class conflict? The answer is not at all that simple, however, and we had best avoid snap conclusions. Nor should we be too quick to rationalize the internal structure of classes, assuming mistakenly that the inequality of power potential among economic, status, and political pyramids "naturally" forces people to try to even out their total power positions.

I have asked that the major components of our political analysis not yet be joined. Let me now extend the request by asking that their internal parts be allowed to move freely by themselves for a moment. I might reinforce this request by pointing out that the Weberian tripartite class hypothesis has never been fully tested empirically. Although it "talks" easily and naturally, it has not yet "researched" very well. It is extremely difficult to examine such an ideologically freighted subject as class in the first place, and, as I have said, even more difficult to conceive of a measure of power potential without evoking overtones of values, institutional loci, and their relations in theories of status and role. In any event, to know the crude facts of power distribution is not necessarily to know how that power is or will be used. A weakness of class theory is that it has almost invariably made mystical assumptions about the use of power as a simple derivative of the existence of power, an intellectually illicit smuggling of a hidden, intervening variable about human nature.

Mills has made this cautionary statement:

> To understand the occupation, class, and status position of a set of people is not necessarily to know whether or not they (1) will become class-conscious, feeling that they belong together or that they can best realize their rational interests by combining; (2) will have "collective attitudes" of any sort, including those toward themselves, their common situation; (3) will organize themselves or be open to organization by others into associations, movements, or political parties; or (4) will become hostile toward other strata and struggle against them. These social, political, and psychological characteristics may or may not occur on the basis of similar objective situations. In any given case, such possibilities must be explored, and "subjective" attributes *must not be used as criteria* for class inclusion, but rather, as Max Weber has made clear, stated as probabilities on the basis of objectively defined situations.[3]

In other words, we must know certain other factual elements in the case or cases under study before we can judge the probable importance of class factors. What Weber suggests is that at the very least we have to add valorative factors to the class factors. This is a key clue and not an isolated hunch, for Weber defines a social event as the combination of an empirical occurrence (an earthquake, a revolution, an elec-

---

[3] Irving Louis Horowitz, ed., *Power, Politics, and People* (New York: Ballantine Books, 1964), p. 320.

tion, or a power failure) and the value significance with which the actors, no matter how far removed, imbue it. Hence, the "fact" of class does not become a "social fact" until we know whether, and then how, class may be perceived by the persons relevant to the situation concerned. For example, most Europeans "see" classes. This perception builds a series of expectations, practices, and predictions into social interaction, which, in general, is reinforced by the relative "realism" of the perception—a reasonable relation between expectation of happenings and actual happenings. On the contrary, most "mainstream" Americans do not "see" classes. Small wonder they are so surprised by revelations of poverty in America, and small wonder they have found it easy to apply racial explanations to the problems of slums, while class interpretations are so easily dismissed.

Social Values

That a man is what he thinks himself to be is a deeply engrained American attitude, and of course it is precisely this "subjective" approach against which Mills warns us in Weber's name. To declare oneself an astronaut is not to be one; no more does one become a member of a class by subjective declaration. There are jails for people who declare themselves to be physicians or policemen without the proper badges, but there need not be such drastic punishment for social mislabeling, unless it is done by social scientists, of course.[4] In any

[4] Weber also warns researchers against ascribing significance to the empirical facts themselves, rather than to the values imposed by the investigator. I made this point earlier in the text, when pointing out the relationship between my own value assumptions and the emphasis I

event, what a person thinks he is certainly has a connection with what he does; but he will still be limited in what he can do by his objective class position, by the perceptions of others, and by other elements we shall come to later.

Now let us be specific about a possible way of grouping values. As a social "law" or "principle" we can say that all people will try to rationalize and justify the way they make sense of their social situation. But "law" cannot tell us what parts of their situation they will perceive, what rationalizing schemes they will generate, and into what contradictions they will fall. These are empirical questions. Our present task, then, is to suggest the kind of categorical system that will guide us in collecting and tagging values relevant to politics in all societies. In this undertaking we will have little use for specific attitudes on parties and personalities, or even ideological stances such as Liberalism, Conservatism, Anarchism, or what have you. Such concepts as the "f-scale," designed to

---

have put on historical uniqueness and the divisibility of class, values, institutions, and individual factors. Weber says:

> We have designated as "cultural sciences" those disciplines which analyze the phenomena of life in terms of their cultural significance. The *significance* of a configuration of cultural phenomena and the basis of this significance cannot however be derived and rendered intelligible by a system of analytical laws . . . , however perfect it may be, since the significance of cultural events presupposes a *value-orientation* toward these events. The concept of culture is a *value*-concept. Empirical reality becomes "culture" to us because and insofar as we relate it to value items. It includes those segments and only those segments of reality which have become significant to us because of this value-relevance. (*The Methodology of the Social Sciences*, tr. and ed. by Edward A. Shils and Henry A. Finch [Glencoe, Ill.: The Free Press, 1949], p. 76.)

This value-relationship guiding "seeing" is as true for the individual in his society as for the social scientist in his sub-culture. The latter, however, has the added obligation of attempting to plumb the bases for his own ascriptions of significance as well as those of his subjects of study.

measure authoritarian personality casts,[5] are at the level of generalization I have in mind—that is, the level of *Weltanschauung*, the basic world-view, how a person sees his social universe when the chips are down and he has discarded all the cards representing politeness, deference, and routine comportment.

In my earlier comments about class I used the development from less complex to more complex systems as a rather amorphous way of emphasizing the complexity of class in contrast to the relative simplicity of basic stratification. Let us reintroduce this opposition of simple to complex and attempt to imagine the basic value stances appropriate to one or the other. We can hypothesize what would be an "appropriate" or "realistic" value system for relatively primitive and elaborate social organizations, and we can also assume that in any situation some explanatory systems will be at work. What we cannot hypothesize, without much more historical information, is what kind of value-system will accompany what kind of social organization in any given set of cases. We can, instead, array value-systems along a scale; at one end we will have those that imbue simple, institutionally undifferentiated (let us say, traditional) societies with sufficiently realistic meaning to support their maintenance; at the other end will be those that imbue highly differentiated, specialized, and complex (let us say, for the time being, modern) societies with meaning sufficient for *their* maintenance.

In a traditional value-system:

—The motivation for decision is ritualistic. ("What was good enough for my father is good enough for me.")

—The effect of any single human action is universal. All

[5] See T. W. Adorno, Else Frenkel-Brunswik, D. J. Levinson, and R. N. Sanford, *The Authoritarian Personality* (New York: Harper, 1950).

action is both secular and sacred; sanctions are both civil and religious: every act has a universal referent. ("Life is a single ball of wax.")

—Change is evil. ("If God wanted us to fly, He would have given us wings.")

And in a modern value-system:

—The motivation for decision is rationalistic. Experimentation and pragmatism are proper modes for searching for desired results. ("Practice makes perfect.")

—The effect of any single human action is relative. What we do in one situation is not necessarily what we should do in others. The separation of church and state helps both institutions. ("One man's meat is another's poison." "Every man's home is his castle.")

—Change is inevitable and should be anticipated and adjusted to. This recognition in itself guides the paths of change. ("This is a world of self-fulfilling prophecy.")

The traditional value-set predisposes in favor of the acceptance of order and authority. Dogma reinforced by rite is, then, an appropriate justification for behavior throughout unchanging time. Indeed, such a posture is necessary for the acceptance of ultimate values of any kind, whether they be religious or ethical in nature. In contrast, the modern value-set embraces partialities—limited and changing orders, as well as the relative merits of accepting transitory authority. Reasonable grounds are considered sufficient for action, which in turn is justifiable only by its plausibility for motivating further action choices. This normative posture well serves the functioning of changing societies, especially industrially urbanized nation-states. But it does not follow that the latter can be run only by persons holding modern values, nor is it the case that all persons in traditional societies hold traditional values. Nor may we suppose that individuals will be either modern or traditional with respect to all their activities and all their institutional and social situations. Quite the contrary; experience suggests that in contemporary societies all kinds of mixtures will be found between situations and value-systems of complexity and simplicity, and that individuals will show complex value patterns within themselves, patterns which will vary through their life careers.

The age of a person can govern his avowal of norms. For example, grammar-school children, close to the embrace of the family and not yet functioning as autonomous individuals, are likely to think in terms of unity, stability, the validity of parental authority, and so forth. When they reach a degree of mature liberation, many people turn to rationalism and relativism and changefulness as criteria of the desirable. It is also likely that many people will value the institutions symbolizing private security in the traditional mode throughout their lives, and that they will prefer the set of institutions which represent adulthood's public striving to be open and changing. An individual may therefore value the family and religion in traditional terms, and education and the economy in modern terms; this "asymmetry" may well keep him more comfortable than if he were to hold similar normative views across the entire institutional array. Politics conceived as an overarching institution that embraces decision and disagreement in all spheres, may then well induce great normative ambivalence when institutional legitimacy and practice become public issues. The bitterness of the history of church-state relations is a case in point. Given the synthetic function of national polities, there is good reason to think that traditional attitudes toward politics may be more resistant to change than attitudes toward any other institutional area.

Examples of disjunction between the social values of political leaders and the societies they attempt to manipulate are easy to find. The governments of many Middle Eastern Islamic countries have assumed that traditionalist officers and soldiers accustomed to an ascriptive system of hierarchy can employ the armaments of a modern society in a modern way. The government of the United States has found it difficult to accept the evidence that weapons of World War II vintage can be manipulated by Asian soldiers who work individualistically, anticipate changes in enemy tactics, and find relativistic answers to difficult questions by substituting bodies for machinery, bicycles for trucks, and tunnels for battlements. In Guatemala the Arbenz government ignored the facts of its world when it tried to apply a Marxist solution to its political problems with a people that could not be recruited to any national level of consensus because they saw their world as a village, or tribal, affair. The Castro Marxists found a population with weak traditional roots and almost without national ties; their job of constructing a national order in Cuba was much easier than the Arbenz regime's task of breakdown and replacement.

Cases of disjunction between values and general social situations abound. The *political* difference such asymmetry makes is another question we had best put aside for the moment. The reason for caution is once again obvious: we have often heard that if ideologies do not change, or if the attitudes of rulers do not change, or if this or that shift in values does not occur, then we are all doomed. I suggest the proper riposte is "sometimes yes, sometimes no." When we begin to assemble the pieces of our model, we shall attempt to determine when each "sometimes" might be anticipated.

Institutional Structure

Institutions are a critical component of political analysis, for they are the "power train"—to use an automotive term—of politics. Through institutions power is made manifest, and the raw power of individuals and of groups is turned into applied power. This statement is as true for the "powerless" as for the most powerful. For example, any "powerless" individual's minimum power can be revealed by his withdrawal from participation. For the withdrawal to be recognized and to have effects requires institutional devices—the communications system, and then all the sub-agencies of the state. Other institutional spheres may also be called into play, ranging from wifely disapproval to the beating up of the recalcitrant's children by schoolmates, from anonymous telephone calls from vigilantes to the loss of his livelihood. The power of the aristocrat, too, is transformed from potential to applied energy only when he purchases his automobile, hires a lobbyist, runs for political office, leaves money to a university, or otherwise puts himself within the structures of applied social activity.

Institutions are thus the subject of most political discussion, even by functionalists. When countries get into trouble, it is their institutions that are said to be crumbling. When changes are urged, articles are written about "new politics and old institutions." Institutional continuity is a sign of stability, and that's good. Institutional breakdown is a sign of instability, and that's bad.

Institutions are sets of routinized behavior patterns that cluster about the performance of certain functions or groups of functions. They are not buildings or groups of men, although they may be symbolized by mortar and flesh. An institution is simply a general, collective way of doing something—within limits normatively defined as acceptable, and with the accompaniment of sanctions if those limits are violated. Institutions are also socializing mechanisms, so that the discharge of an institution's functions can be maintained even though the actors change. Last, they are control mechanisms. They may be decentralized in organization, as is the family or religion in a multi-sect society like that of the United States. Or, decentralized actions may be focused in highly centralized and visible structures, as in a bourse or a legislature.

The more formal structures develop within broad institutions, the more we talk about bureaucracies and about institutions taking on a life of their own and becoming divorced from the accomplishment of general social functions. The long-standing American argument over the national purpose is an example of the disquiet generated when it seems that the formal structures of politics are becoming autonomous and no longer responsive to the general political institution —that cluster of routinized activities which performs the functions of settling disputes which the common consent places in the public domain, of establishing policy, representing interests, allocating some of society's rewards and punishments, and so on. To take an example, President Johnson, in pursuing his Vietnam policy, banked on a politics of general consensus. His opponents argued that, on the contrary, consensus broke down to such an extent that the government was administering national policy as though the American people were the enemy. Sometimes the reply was that if the people only understood what was at stake, most of them would support the policy unequivocally. (The last gasp of this line of protestation is, "History will absolve me!") The counter-reply was that the government's dissemination of partial information or misinformation prevented this consensus, and that the government's argument confused loyalty to the officers of government with loyalty to the social institution of the polity. And there it was: the confusion of the general institution with its specific and necessarily temporary guardians vitiated any recognition of a truly public interest and weakened both the political institution and its formal organization.

If institutions are clusters of routinized behavior patterns, it is also true that some people routinely discharge given behavior patterns more intensely than other people do. These differences in a person's relation to an institution reflect a difference in the definition of the functions to be performed, an effect of institutional durability and human bodily fragility. Institutions are inherited from the past but must function today. The fit of past and present sometimes pinches. It was in full recognition of this fact that Jefferson proposed a revolution for every generation. It also explains why the Mexicans cry for free suffrage and a limitation of the presidency to one term, and why personalistic French politics is a threat to institutional continuity.

Once again, I am not suggesting that this analysis is particularly new, but the examples offered within the pattern of the full presentation may be interesting. Institutions should be thought of not in abstract isolation, but rather in terms of the value significance their actors give them and the class order they make effective. Taking the three together, we may learn which values the institutions in turn propagate, which groups have the best chance of managing them, and what personal success within an institution may have to do with changing the patterns of potential class power for later generations.

These are examples of the maximum necessary or "natural" links, which, to my mind, bind class, values, and institutions. All other questions are empirical and to be answered within each historical situation.

In approaching actual cases, then, the scales of measurement should be the same as the ones we used before: the institution's degree of structural complexity, and the degree of autonomy or differentiation characterizing each. And, again as we did before, let us not presume that these two are always synonymous or even correlated. Totalitarian societies are built on the premise that very high orders of specialization, and thus of complexity, should be subsumed under an all-encompassing political structure, which effectively inhibits institutional differentiation. Indeed, we call such societies "totalitarian" precisely because they stand the individual citizen up straight and naked before the state, with no intervening and arbitrating structures in which he can hide. Families are to breed for the good of the nation, the economy is to be organized for the same purpose, education inculcates worship of the Fatherland, and God (as is usual with man) is pressed into the service of aggrandizing the state. The final turn is taken when the citizen is told that politics is the duty of the governor only. Perón consistently made this point to his Argentine *descamisados,* telling them that in his role as "First Worker" it was his responsibility to decide, theirs to support and obey. He added that they were lucky to avoid his headaches.

Complexity and differentiation are often seen as being about the same thing, because the usual continuum of political development is thought of as running from the unspecialized structures of primitive society to the highly specialized ones of modern, industrial society. Since differentiation is found only where there is specialization, the two are often regarded as synonymous. What I am saying, instead, is that institutional specialization is a necessary but insufficient condition for differentiation, which also presupposes some form of pluralism—the relative freedom of one institution from the influence of power figures fostered by another. For instance, to have money is fine and may even be fun, but, after all, one man one vote. In addition, with true differentiation the values attached to the performance of one set of activities should not necessarily affect others. We may think that country people are nicer than city people, but state legislatures should not permit the weight of one rural voice to be worth ten urban ones. Again, one man one vote.

Unfortunately, some forms of differentiation bode ill for the development of well-knit societies. While specialization and differentiation grow for some individuals or groups in a nation, negative distinctions may evolve for others: ethnic differences may be used to exclude some of the people from participating in certain institutions; class differences may muscle others aside. Ethical and ideological disaffections may distinguish not only among patterns of behavior within a single institution, but among the ways that types of communities manage to coexist within the larger society; the behavior exhibited by the alienated classes or normatively disaffected segments will differ from that of the institutionally integrated population.

In many countries of the world "colored" populations are denied access to the institutions controlled by the superordinate population. They are told to live in an undifferentiated situation with few links to the society's institutions, while the "sanctified" proceed to construct their own universes of living and dying, doing and undoing, believing and disbelieving. This exclusion is commonly reinforced by arguments that qualitatively the *Untermenschen* are different kinds of human beings. Let them sing and dance with their odd and exciting rhythms; they do not care about growth and death, and they are stupid and insensitive. The line of justification is that the complex institutional structure of the "ins" must be closed to the "outs" because the latter cannot be expected to learn required behavior patterns and normatively acceptable explanations.

Exclusion on the basis of class or race may not always reach the extremes of the Nazi Final Solution, but the ideological justification for it is always in the same family of events. The organizational problem is essentially one of relating class to institutions, and it can be solved either by giving the outsiders access to the institutions or by their physical removal.

Self-withdrawal because one's values (or one's group's values) are incompatible with institutional practice is quite another matter. Many members of the New Left throughout the world profess to see little positive meaning in the institutions of western countries, whether democratic-capitalistic or Soviet-Communist. They are alienated, however, not from an economic situation, but from the basic tools of social organization, finding their nations' institutions irrelevant to their life purposes, to their basic value postulates. This withdrawal cuts right through entire institutional systems, ripping across the whole array of a society's institutions and removing an entire group from participation in them. Examples of such voluntary withdrawal are much rarer than the exclusion mechanisms of ethnic and class segregation.

Personal Behavior

When we include personal characteristics in social-science analysis, we enormously complicate our data. A usual remedy is to define the problem away on the ground that the social sciences deal with groups of persons and not with individuals, with probabilities and not statistical "sports." Still, an adequate political science must somehow tame the matter of personal temper and ability, as the following newspaper report sharply reminds us:

> Saturday, Dec. 3, 1966, was a quiet day in Foggy Bottom —just the right kind of day for the secret, technical preparations underway in the State Department, the culmination of five months' quiet diplomacy, leading to peace negotiations to end the war in Vietnam.
>
> Sitting down to breakfast, looking forward to the last-minute arrangements of the day, a senior official in the national-security apparatus opened his morning paper and gasped as he read the headline: U.S. BOMBS SITE 5 MILES FROM HANOI. "Oh my God," he muttered. "We lost control." The official shock grew from the fact that a foreign capital had been bombed, and the President and his top civilian lieutenants had forgotten that they had authorized it.[6]

The skeptic might say that the forgetfulness was Freudian, that duplicity was governing the situation. But there is no reason for not taking the story at face value: there was a human slip, encouraged by all-too-human characteristics—de-

[6] Review by David Schoenbrun of David Kraslow and Stuart H. Loory, *The Secret Search for Peace in Vietnam* (New York: Random House, 1968), in *The New York Times Book Review,* July 7, 1968, p. 1.

sire for secrecy, desire for personal control, pride. How can incidents like this one be subjected to political analysis so that even minimal predictability is possible? Whatever we say, let us recognize that no such incident can possibly be predicted; all we can foresee are the fields in which they are likely to occur.

There are three politically relevant aspects of personality type: competence (interest, intelligence, energy level, and so on); empathic ability to see into the lives and thoughts of others who are removed by social distance; and individual desires and styles, conditioned by the limits society sets on its leaders, brokers, followers, and pariahs. The last is the connective tissue between individual characteristics and society at large, and it takes us from a mere examination of idiosyncrasy to the study of fields of variation.

Individual traits and abilities are the characteristics that most citizens discuss when they consider candidates for public office. They wonder whether an aspirant has the trustworthiness of a used-car salesman, or the ability to direct a massive administration; whether one candidate is a megalomaniac, another overly ambitious; whether there is too much "smoothness" or evidence of family instability. The fact that television reveals personal traits perhaps more fully than any other news medium has a great deal to do with its reputation as a determinant in American politics. The famous analysis of the late Senator Joseph McCarthy's televised hearings into activities of the U.S. Army is a case in point: to say that the Senator alienated the public because he resembled the heavies in TV Westerns is to state, in effect, that the content of the problem was irrelevant and that the personal revelations were all-important. A close analogy is afforded by the common assessment of the debates between Richard M. Nixon and John F. Kennedy in 1960. Was Nixon's failure then but the failure of his make-up men?

The perception of traits is one important element in political success; their actual possession is equally important, however. An extremely wealthy scion of an aristocratic family whose personal values are known to be libertarian and who is at the same time sybaritic, lazy, and uninterested in politics will probably never exercise his potential power in government, though he may succeed in having his parking tickets fixed. It will no doubt be difficult even to induce him to donate more than token amounts to political parties. A person of similar station and values who has a burning ambition for political life but is handicapped by poor intellectual endowment can almost certainly find himself a niche, even if only as the appointed member of some obscure commission; depending on circumstances, he may well be able to win elective office. Under these conditions, the possible range of his behavior in given situations will not be impossible to foresee.[7]

In rough terms, intellectual capacity is to the individual as class is to society, a personal estimate of potential for public behavior. Clearly, however, we cannot jump from an estimate of a person's capacity to an inference about his social actions. We need a bridge between capacity as a purely personal matter and the ability to socialize thought—to be sensitive to the worlds of others, to permit one's own world to be influenced by others, and to affect others in determinate and deliberate ways. It is not enough, then, to know a person's abilities or even his abilities plus his felt wants and "natural"

[7] Harold D. Lasswell has gone far toward organizing these and other manifestations of behavior in many of his books, particularly in *Psychopathology and Politics* (rev. ed., New York: The Viking Press, 1960).

needs; we also need to know his social capacities before we can even begin to "place" him.

Much new knowledge has been provided on this subject during the past generation. Daniel Lerner, for example, in his classical *The Passing of Traditional Society*,[8] speaks of empathy as a major characteristic of modern man, by which he means a person's ability to "see" psychologically across social distance, to put himself in someone else's shoes. Empathy in more or less undifferentiated "face-to-face" societies is an easy and not very significant social task. In complex and differentiated modern societies, it is an ability of a much higher order, and it is of great importance in overriding class and ethnic distinctions, among others, in national societies. It also has its uses in new nations attempting to build upon the variegated base of multi-tribal organization; leaders who cannot or will not bring empathy into play are likely to regret its absence, as the tragic history of Nigeria demonstrates all too appallingly.

Philip Converse deals with the same issue by asking what spread or breadth of symbols a single symbolic stimulus triggers.[9] The usefulness of this question is that its answer can tell us which kinds of people are likely to become political men and which will not. At one end of the scale is the complete ideologue, the man who would ask the existential question of a rusted nail. Mention apple pie to him, for example, and he will think of coffee, which will lead him to how badly his mother-in-law brews coffee, to the time when his brother-in-law dropped out of school because of the bad family back-

[8] Daniel Lerner, *The Passing of Traditional Society* (2nd. ed., New York: The Free Press, 1958).
[9] Philip Converse, "The Nature of Belief Systems in Mass Publics," in David Apter, ed., *Ideology and Discontent* (New York: The Free Press, 1964), pp. 206-261.

ground, and how the family life was poisoned because his
father-in-law lost his job and committed suicide, and how
evil the system is that permits unemployment, and the kind
of exploitation which will pay coffee pickers and sugar grow-
ers less than a dollar a day for their work, and all of this is
why Brazilians have a military government to keep the workers down, but, even so, Castro is not to be excused for trading
American for Russian imperialists, but in the long run they'll
all fall prey to their own crassness. At the other end of the
scale is the poor fellow who, when you mention apple pie,
thinks of apple pie. As can be imagined, a person's position
on this scale strongly reflects the effects of his education and
training—his capacity, areas of interest, skill, and knowledge. The spread of symbolic referents is an elegant addition to Lerner's empathy concept, for it permits the notion of ability-to-project to be refined so that one can consider
how far the empathic projection goes, in which direction (or
directions), whether simultaneously or serially, and with what
richness of detail and connotation.

Another facet of the same issue has been polished by social
psychologists working in the area of communications. One
subject of inquiry among these scholars concerns the way in
which people infuse the same, or apparently the same, symbols with different factual and emotional content. Understanding how subjective factors may color the most "objective" of data is enormously important to anyone using ques-
tionnaires in research, for example; the rankest amateur
knows that persons in differing groups (sometimes even in
the same group) may well understand the same question in
extraordinarily different ways. The noise thus disturbing
communication among persons and across groups is obvious.
"Free education" in a Catholic culture, for example, means

not at all the same thing as it does in the United States. For a Latin American, "free education" refers to the legal ability of religiously sponsored schools to give valid degrees—a meaning substantively opposite to the American one. This simple case of dissonance is but a whispered echo of the racket that erupts when someone asks the meaning of "peace-keeping," or "democratic," or even "constitutional right to bear arms." The emotional charges accompanying these words may also vary, touching off accusations of "coldness" or "over-reaction" or what have you, when mutual understanding is slight. All societies develop elaborate sets of signals so that people may know when this kind of multiple understanding and reacting is taking place. The signals are better understood by the empathetic than by the insensitive, and their content can better be judged by an empathetic person who can string information together than by one whose ability to build connotative chains is low.

Cognizance of these personal characteristics and abilities is clearly important when we study the elite in a society, when we try to discern why some people emerge from their class and value positions to assume leadership positions. It is equally important, I believe, to an understanding of the quality of "followership." Class interpretations of leader-follower relations abound, of course, especially in analyses of nazi, fascist, and other right-wing movements—Nazism as an alliance between certain upper-class and lower middle-class elements, Italian fascism as a kind of middle-class developmentalist response to problems posed by modernizing pluralism. Other interpretations refine the class analysis by pointing out that individuals and groups who seek mystical and authoritarian solutions to their problems are behaving not only as members of a class but as people who feel their status threatened (the uppers because they are not accorded the prestige appropriate to their economic weight, and the lower middle-class groups because they are menaced by rising elements from semi-skilled and unskilled labor and by ethnically disparate persons). Nevertheless, I continue to feel that a gap exists in these interpretations; still missing is the element explaining why some lower-class persons did not follow Perón's banner in Argentina, why there were anti-fascist partisans in Italy, often led by people from the same class groups as those who followed Mussolini, and why some *nouveaux riches* spend their money to support racial integration and left-wing causes.

In explaining leader-follower relations partially on the basis of personal qualities, we should not neglect the force of simple intelligence and reason. "Feel" can be tempered by logic, and often is. Many American intellectuals, for instance, found it very difficult to understand how in 1964 Barry Goldwater could promise to pursue military preparedness and the Vietnam war, and simultaneously balance the budget. Questioning his mental competence, they of course remained entirely unavailable to Republican blandishments. A lack of consistency between promises, or between promises and action, creates credibility gaps for some and simply fortifies doctrine for others. Followers vary in their level of political interest and knowledge, their ability to see into others' problems, and their competence to synthesize the available bits and scraps of political information. In combination these personal attributes predispose them to accept or reject one or another of the styles and varieties of leadership offered them. We cannot give ourselves the luxury of presuming that these choices will necessarily be less personalistic and more rational in industrialized states. The cult of Stalin flourished in an industrially developing country, and Hitler peddled his charisma in what was one of the most highly industrialized, urbanized, and literate societies in the world. Smudging the line between secrecy for the sake of national security and covertness for the sake of political party security has created an immense credibility gap in the United States, where political rationalism is by no means as advanced as industrial rationalization.

I have discussed personal competence and "empathy" as politically relevant personal factors, mentioning leader-follower relations as one of the ways in which these factors enter politics. The bridge between the entirely personal and the collectively probabilistic has other building materials: the understanding of symbols across social distance as well as within the same strata; the configuration of content, symbol, and behavior that we call "style," and how these styles are attractive, neutral, or repellent; the range of surface differences acceptable to total societies or groups, and so on. The leadership-followership relation is useful to the theorist in providing a strategic way of linking individual actions to collective occurrences. Another link, having to do with normative matters, comprises ideological systems and personally held ideologies.

Let us define ideology as a verbalized (or verbalizable), polemical set of ideas concerning the meaning of life in past, present, and future manifestations. Ideologies are rationalizations. They are *conscious* ways of special pleading—as contrasted with values, which are deep-seated and silent except in profound crises that strip us and leave us bare to the skin of our primary social animalhood. Ideologies are constructed out of our conscious learning experiences. Values are more mysterious in their origins, perhaps in part inherited, if

psychological stance can be inherited, but certainly incul-
cated as part of our early socialization. I have placed ideologies in this discussion of personal factors in politics, then,
because they are part of the political payoff of capacities and
empathic abilities and assumed political relationships. They
are held by persons in groups, but their acceptance or rejection is an act subject to personal will. An individual can shrug
off an ideology; his class origins or world-view are not so
easily shucked.

Analytical refinement demands that we separate values
from ideologies. Unless we do so, certain problems defy satisfactory explanation. One problem, for example, comes to us
in the information we have on formal education and attitude
change. There seem to be two contradictory sets of conclusions. The better-known results inform us time and again
that education correlates positively with tolerance, internationalism, awareness of the problems of others, and so
forth, down the road of classical American liberal politics;
for instance, the longer a student stays at Harvard, the more
likely he is to espouse the politics of the Democratic Party.
Yet other data suggest that education does little to change
attitudes: the person who is of authoritarian cast when he
starts his education stays unchanged. Those who are made
mobile by education end up thinking like the people in the
group toward which they have moved, but very likely they
were preconditioned to think like the members of the group
they wanted to be in. In these apparently contradictory findings we may be measuring two different phenomena: explicit idea-systems and implicit value sets, the former change-
able, the latter resistant to change. But we must be very cau-
tious in advancing this possibility, for it is yet to be demonstrated.

New Left and confrontation politics also suggest that we should discriminate between ideological convictions and personality sets. Many puzzled critics of the intransigence evidenced in the politics of confrontation denounce it as fascist. And certainly some attributes of confrontationists fit that definition: the participants' conviction that they are the vessels of absolute truth, their disdain for anything but total rejection of the "system," their use of verbal violence and advocacy of physical violence, and their yearnings for organic "community." Yet their avowed purpose is not the advancement of fascism; they espouse love and togetherness, an end to exploitation and anomie, the creation of a truly free society geared to individual desire, and the importance of learning as a private experience geared to personal activism. They seem to be authoritarian in basic attitudes and in much of their behavior, yet libertarian in ideology. We may add that their social origins are not similar to those of European fascists, nor is there anything fascist-like about the social situations of the groups with which they seek alliance.

In personal matters, we can expect to find human beings living very comfortably with manifold and obvious inconsistencies—the gentle man who becomes a tiger behind the wheel of his car, or the civil-libertarian merchant who gouges customers in his store, or the fighter for free enterprise who devotes his life to building a monopoly. Indeed, there are consequences to these counterposed attitudes and behavior patterns, and they do not occur accidentally. The burden of my argument, then, is not that we are in a chaotic world of infinite possibilities, but that the probabilities are greater than we may have allowed for. And what social scientists see as a "natural" order may be the product of too narrow a definition of consistency, and too narrow a view of man's ability to accommodate contradictions.

Our task for the remainder of this book will be to suggest some ways of putting order into diversity or seeming disparity, while keeping the generalizations at a level that will comfortably accommodate the realities of social practice. No attempt will be made to enter into the fine details of how the analytical elements interact. Instead, I shall choose two major areas of inquiry, that of conflict and that of the conditions of public freedom, and will sketch out possible approaches to their understanding.

This chapter has been by way of a rediscovery of political elements common to political thinkers throughout almost all history since the Renaissance. If I have added something new, it is in insisting on the difference between naturally necessary relations and those that must be empirically demonstrated in each political case. Only by understanding the difference between the inevitable and the manipulable can we realize all the possibilities that are ours in the political realm.

■■ Conflict and Reconciliation

Concerning social change and causation,
and levels of conflict; with a short treatise
on the identification of the enemy

I doubt that any total, scientifically defensible, dynamic model of social change can be constructed at this time. Certainly, I cannot construct one. But I will attempt to present a static model of change and suggest limited causal explanations. That is, I will try to plot possible courses of social change, moving from one dot to another through patterns of conflict and resolution. A truly dynamic theory would not merely map the courses of change in this way, but would also fill in the precise trajectories from dot to dot, revealing the generically causal forces as well as the historically specific ones. But hypotheses about ultimate causations, and their relationship to given motor elements, escape our ability to validate and fall outside the body of scientific knowledge. To stretch for an unprovable total explanation before exhausting the efforts to provide more limited causal explanations is in any event more religious than scientific in motive. So I suggest we talk about change and causality in limited time spans of human activity, without trying to relate the causes of social change to Human Nature or any other absolute or mystical concepts.

The leap from absolute premise to specific social conclusion is often accomplished by jumping over social life. Homeostatic or tension-management theories are examples of theories suffering from this fault, as I have mentioned. For example, we might construct this chain of change and cause: false information given to policy-makers leads to false predictions; members of the polity then perceive a resulting failure of policy; they develop tensions caused by the discrepancy between anticipated and actual results, between the previous explanations and the new ones; action to alleviate the tension must occur; if all goes well, a new balance is attained. Now, it is tempting to fit political action into tidy models like this one, but a causal chain of this sort presumes and neglects too much.

Many theorists of the "tension school" have recognized the weaknesses in their approach, especially its failure to take into account that some people are better able to perceive tension-inducing mechanisms than others, and that some are better able to reduce tensions than others: that is, somewhere along the line, capacities and power should be stirred into the theory. "Tension-management" theory has been designed to take care of that problem by showing that leaders are institutionally delegated the power to perceive contradictions, to act on their perceptions, and to redress balance in the appropriate way. But the only basic change advanced in this elaboration is a curt nod in the direction of class, bureaucracy, or whatever other power measure the observer may be employing. That disjunction actually does cause tension has still not been demonstrated; nor do we know what relates a recognition of tension to subsequent action, or what influences affect the action. We have no way of knowing the differences between the judgment of the tension-managers and the actual facts of the situation; the managers may well try to manipulate social "facts" that exist only in their own fertile imaginations. In truth, political leaders constantly try to resolve crises that cannot be pressed into the forms of their perceptions, or else are not susceptible to the solutions they propose.

Homeostatic theories are also logically treacherous: they tempt us to make ingenious after-the-fact analyses. Assuming that tension leads to action, how do we know how *much* tension is required to produce activity? If the spur bites too deep, why not simply give up, or go manic? If the spur merely tickles, why not endure, or enjoy it? Or does the level of tension have to be "just right," like Toynbee's challenge-and-response theory? Retrospectively, one can point out that for a long time things were "just right" for the Romans but eventually became too much for them. Why and how? That remains for stronger theories to unravel.

Another difficulty with theories of self-adjustment is that they do not adequately account for the possibility that sometimes balance simply cannot be redressed within the existing system, that some social situations demand new and different systems to attain equilibrium. In other words, these theories do not adequately handle revolution. To say only that revolutionary change is "qualitative," merely another if more difficult manner of re-establishing equilibrium, glosses over the conditions for and processes of change. Such an Olympian view practically voids an examination of different kinds of tensions as they affect persons and groups, of the moments when tensions become intolerable to some. To treat cases of almost total institutional breakdown, which is what some revolutions are, as simply incidents along the way to tension-resolution is like playing *Die Zauberflöte* on a Jew's harp.

These equilibrium theories typify a much larger class of political thought. Similar points of view have been around for a long time, from the Epicureans and Hedonists to the British Utilitarians and Bentham's calculus of pleasures and pains. Theories of economic man and his self-correcting market mechanisms offer a more sophisticated explanation than most treatises on the golden mean, because the classical liberal view of economics spells out a full set of relations between the intrinsic human naturalness of certain kinds of conduct and the institutions ideally appropriate to reinforce such conduct—thus taking a giant step beyond theories that jump directly from human nature to conduct. Nevertheless, even natural-man-plus-natural-institutions presumes more than is necessary for analysis, and more than is helpful in connecting normative theory to behavior.

Although many others before me have questioned grand theories based on human nature, the theorist must not disown his human nature; at some point in his exposition every theorist should make explicit his act of faith. But I shall try to postpone a statement of my own commitment for as long as possible, and to make it of minimal importance to the judgment of the remainder of the work. My purpose here is to go as far as possible in explanation before reaching for the undemonstrable, to reveal the intricate synapses of social behavior with a minimum of blind leaps. While avoiding metaphysical, ontological, and teleological questions at this point, I do not want to imply that structuring the elements of politics through conflict and conciliation situations is the only way to understand political purposes and patterns. Polities are channels for social organization and mobilization, as well as for creating and resolving conflict. Segments of a political system—pressure groups, political parties, the government itself—create ideas and proposals for change as well as receive them. Governments train people, in and out of schools, and organize the carrying out of functions, from cutting forest trails to delivering the mail. I have chosen to emphasize conflict and conciliation for reasons of tactical convenience, not strategic necessity; this focus is a fairly efficient way of showing interactions that make for the political expression of power, legitimacy, authority, and consensus.

I will permit myself another digression. One omission from the typology of conflict to be presented here demands explanation from the start. I do not take class conflict as a single category of conflict, let alone as the causal element in social change. Class is certainly an element in conflict and conciliation situations, but the use of class power to defend class-defined interests, and the life-styles that contribute to this use, are matters that can be understood only in relation to value systems, institutions, and personal factors. By treating the class concept as one that describes the distribution of raw energy, I do not mean to reify it. Rather, I wish to demystify it by using it as a power measure, valid through time, and given social significance only through normative, institutional, and personal factors. The ideological contention that class consciousness is always related to class conflict is denied by experience, as Marx himself, the father of the idea, saw with entire clarity.

Marx . . . did not expect there to be a high correlation between objective class position and subjective revolutionary class consciousness until the point at which the social system broke down: if there was to be total class consciousness in any given society, then by definition it would be in the midst of revolution. In normal times, structural factors press deprived strata to become conscious, but the inherent strength of the ruling class prevents class consciousness . . . and . . . is able to "buy off" those inclined to lead or participate in opposition movements. The Marxist term that characterizes the ideology of the lower class in the period of the predominance of the other classes is "false consciousness." [1]

The term "false consciousness" implies that there is an extra-social criterion of "real consciousness," a criterion that can stem only from a value assumption. Vulgar Marxists forget this, however, and often pursue their tactics in the belief that "real" class interests—whether of ruling or of subordinate classes—will always manifest themselves. Marx, as well as his followers, by giving primary attention to class as a divisive influence, also tended to underemphasize the strength of social syntheses—the "real" interest of persons of widely varying social stations in maintaining the integrity of a total system. Small wonder that nationalism, the most important cohesive element in modern society, should have opened breaches between Marxist theoreticians and Marxist politicians. In a trite example of tension between nation and class, the European proletariat failed to band together across frontiers in unified opposition to bourgeois World War I because their normative identification with their national community easily overrode international fellowship with kindred members of their class group. One may argue whether they

[1] Seymour Martin Lipset, *Revolution and Counterrevolution: Change and Persistence in Social Structures* (New York: Basic Books, 1968), pp. 126-27. The chapter from which the quotation is taken, entitled "Issues in Social Class Analysis," is a lucid and wise discussion of the major schools of sociological thought concerning stratification and class.

were politically right or wrong in this choice, but certainly it cannot seriously be said that their attitudes were "false," even to their own "true" interests. For good or ill, their views were authentic enough to lead millions of the men who held them to an early grave. The point is that all consciousness is real,. but some is beneficial, some pernicious, and some irrelevant.

The Alliance for Progress was a peculiar Western Hemisphere version of the same false belief in an implicit "real reality"—this time applied to elites. Latin American leaders were admonished to recognize their "true" interests and reform before it was too late, before the "masses," crazed by the "revolution of rising expectations," rose in class wrath to destroy them. This ethical definition of the "real" interests of Latin America's upper classes made by many North American as well as Latin American leaders was an acceptable and even laudable one. But it did not recognize that there can be no single "real" interest as such unless there is also a generally accepted explanation of the purpose and meaning of life— a social equivalent of the assumptions of good and bad lying behind a formal system of ethics. Otherwise, the definition of interest is a relative, cultural, and individual matter, not necessarily shared, for example, by North American and Latin American elites. Further, to the extent that racial, foreign, and other troubles plague the North American scene, even displays of allegedly "valid" interests that might be held in common have little persuasiveness in Latin America.

Unfortunately, the contemptuous attacks that have been made on the pleas for Latin American reform also reflect fatalistic views of class power. To avow that the Alliance for Progress was bound to fail because Latin aristocracies are immune to reform, since no class has ever willingly given up its prerogatives, is to assume that "prerogatives" and "willingly" and "given up" all have the same meanings no matter what the cultural and historical setting may be. If we assume such an iron law of human conduct, then there is really no way to explain, for example, how the British aristocracy arrived where it is, in contrast to the Spanish aristocracy. Or, to take another example, is it historically valid to say that the American Negro did not begin to see his social condition improve until he began to organize and thus create political power for himself? Certainly without that creation of power, the United States would not be addressing the problem of race with the present sense of urgency. But was there no paving of the Negro's way by more powerful white allies? We can recognize that superordinate groups are loath to surrender their prerogatives, but we need not also assume that they will *always* attempt "final solutions" in their "natural" self-defense. The issue is not, of course, one of a simple, bald, unmodified willingness or refusal to cede or share prerogatives. The issue is, rather, what will the powerful permit themselves to do to those who threaten them? How far will they go in defending their interests? How sensitively do they recognize that the act of defending their interests necessarily changes those interests? To have used atomic bombs in the Dominican Republic, the Congo, Vietnam, or Cuba would certainly have defended American interests as the American government defined them, but it would also have qualitatively changed the definition of what it was we thought we were defending. That is, changes in a social order are worked not only by attacks on the power system, but also by the means used to defend the system. More than a few ruling groups have recognized the possibly self-defeating effect of defending their interests in a way that changes the society they seek to preserve. Unhappily, more than a few have not. The point is that, historically, different choices have been made, proving that man is not the passive creature of his class position.

For these and many other reasons, I cannot consider class conflict as an overarching category that embraces all clashes in modern societies. The influence of social class, where it exists, or of simple social differentiation, is a part of every conflict equation, but it is only sometimes the core of conflict.

Conflict, Interest, and Causality

Having put aside the application of ultimate and universal causality to the analysis of specific cases, we still have the possibility of intermediate levels of social causality.[2] In this limited but still macrocosmic sense, we can share in the implication of most extant theories of social change by saying that whatever makes an event possible "causes" it. This substitution of "possibility" for "causality" is as fitting in the analysis of political affairs as it would be absurd in the natural sciences. We can say that the Fourth French Republic was caused by the weakness of the Third Republic, but to say that the progression was "made possible" by the Third Republic's weakness is empirically more comfortable. On the contrary, to say that the boiling water was "made possible" by the gas flame under the pot is to indulge in undue vagueness. Are atomic explosions "caused" or "made possible by" the attainment of critical mass under certain conditions? Using the verb "cause" in social analysis implies over-pre-

[2] I am not using Robert Merton's "middle-range" theory in a strict sense. I mean only that I omit individual and "human nature" factors in this part of the analysis, staying with groups and communities in historically significant contexts.

cision; using the phrase "make possible" in the natural sciences involves under-precision.

Our urge to advance "natural" causal explanations of social happenings may come out of the wish to emulate the seeming precision of the physical sciences, methodologically committed as they are to defining precise relationships among space-time occurrences. Within physical processes no possibility of autonomous reaction is presumed, for "mind" and "consciousness" are not within the realm of physical inquiry. Thus, saying that physical reactions are "made possible" by external stimuli is a mere euphemism. In human affairs, however, only physiological matters can be given the straight cause-and-effect terminology: "The brain stopped functioning because it was deprived of oxygen," for instance. Otherwise, we must recognize choice as the additional variable, thinking of "causation" as that which makes it possible for individuals, groups, and societies to act as they do.

Now, the most complete way of putting this matter is to say that the necessary and sufficient conditions for a satisfactory social explanation are the sum of these factors: what makes choices possible, plus the effective exercise of choice or the routine following of custom and habit, or a mixture of conscious choice and custom. Most causal explanations in the social sciences rest content with advancing "necessary" conditions—"objective" matters like an economic situation, literacy rate, or the like. Their "sufficiency" must be supplied through an examination of how alternative courses of action are envisioned and selected by the actors involved, or their degree of surrender to habitual modes of response, in addition to a study of the patterns into which the "necessary" elements fall.

The words "causality," "cause," and "causation" will hereafter be used with the qualifications just given. Several additional points should be made, however. First, the more primitive a society in its ability to control its social doings, the more may we use "causation" in a physical-science sense; that is, the more accurately are we speaking of a mechanism that is only reactive. The more rationalized and rationalistic a society, the more can stimuli be internally generated as well as received from the outside, and the more do stimuli "make possible" effective and innovative choices. Second, this definition of social causality is useful only in the limited, non-naturalistic mode of analysis chosen here. If we admit of no engines that must be obeyed *in any particular, given way,* still there certainly are some that we must obey in some way or another if we are to survive physically, and others that we must obey if we are to grow socially. And, third, this approach reinforces a by-now-evident bias: that I see conscious maneuverability as a powerful potential of the human situation. At the risk of indulging in the vice of sentimentally longing for social freedom, I am, of course, moving toward positing the possibility, even necessity, of a rational voluntarism in many areas of the social order.

Let us apply this "causality-possibility" construction to an example, one chosen from the general study of revolution, if only because taking extreme cases is a classical and useful device in political analysis. The apparent paradox that revolutionaries often come from advantaged families has often been noted. Does this higher social status of itself "cause" or make it possible to be a revolutionary? A refined answer requires more elements to be considered. A revolutionary believes that fundamental political change is impossible unless power is generated and accumulated to be used against an existing government, or unless the tacit consent of the citizenry can be withdrawn from that government—or, more often than not, both. For a person to reach those conclusions and persuade others to them, he must have the psychological ability of empathy, and have the information necessary to see realistically into other persons' lives; that is, his empathic ability must not be betrayed by a factual ignorance that would make him sound hollow to his potential supporters. He must also be somewhat predictive, pragmatic in his tactics, and with some access to the institutional structure, at least enough for him to communicate with his potential followers. He may even attempt to build institutional bases parallel to those of the established society. (Clandestine radio stations are an apt example, as are guerrilla paramilitary organizations.)

Individuals with those abilities are usually well educated. They somehow have had time to work out their ideas and the organization of their power—whether in universities, jails, exile, or wherever. They have learned, that is, the range of effective choice—the possible definitions of victory for them, and alternative ways of achieving it. They are then forging ideology. Certainly it is more likely than not that persons who are inclined to take direct, personal action, who possess the "value stances" of changefulness and pragmatism and predictiveness, and who have been formally educated, come from reasonably well-off families. Thus it is not the fact of class that "causes" it all: it is the simultaneous or serial interaction of all the variables that permits the emergence of the revolutionary individual. These variables are only the *necessary* causal elements. *Sufficiency* of explanation is added by the intensity of the elements, and by the configuration of their combination.

Individuals who are able to fill the role of revolutionary

leader can actually do so only if their followers perceive the conflict with sufficient intensity and urgency, and if the channels for conflict-resolution are sufficiently clogged, so that extra-institutional problem-solving seems desirable and necessary, weighed against possible costs. It may be that for societal or personal reasons revolutionaries will appeal only to those in essentially the same position as their own. (Student revolutionaries usually appeal only to fellow students, not to workers.) Or, as is commonly the case, divergent interest groups may combine for the purpose of revolution and separate for the purposes of consolidating post-revolutionary power.[3] In any event, these causal relations need not be analyzed only after the fact. With an adequate collection and analysis of relevant data, the inherent probabilities in given situations can be seen. There is thus a heuristic value in this approach, a guide to the search for relevant data. Once all this information is in hand, revolutionary behavior still cannot be explained without considering how revolutionary leaders and followers make a series of decisions to act—to become revolutionaries in deeds. And, finally, the success of their endeavors (and of our causal analysis) depends in good measure on the mixture of reason and reflex infusing the chains of decisions made by the actors as they move into, through, and beyond the revolutionary process.

This midi-causal analysis, so to speak, does not answer questions such as why societies seem to be on a long drift toward higher orders of complexity and synthesis, or what the ultimate purpose of the human experience may be, if anything at all. Still, it can go far toward helping us understand how it was, for example, that invention and technological innovation in traditional China failed to bring about the

[3] This suggests the possible range of effective charisma.

growth of a scientific establishment, and it can give us clues to the understanding of the interaction in Western Europe among such massive changes as Protestantism, science, capitalism, and representative democracy. We will not learn "why" generic social change as such occurs, but we can learn much about why and how relatively specific and historically bounded changes occur. This claim demands more than its mere assertion. In the next chapter, the technique will be tested on questions of this order of generality.

Let us turn to conflict and its resolution as one way of analyzing a set of political interactions, and also, of course, to test our ability to fit the analytical elements into a synthetic whole.

For the present purpose, a brief definition of political conflict will do: it is any overt clash involving all or some of a political institution, motivated by perceived interest differences among the parties with some power to act. To use the expression "perceived interest" is not an underhanded way of introducing a governing *deus ex machina.* "Perceived interest" is merely a sub-category of valorative and ideological elements, having to do with whether persons and groups prize or despise something enough to be willing to fight over it.

Value Conflict

The most profound and most significant conflicts grow out of clashes between different or opposing value systems. Groups of people with conflicting world-views imbue institutions and all other social interactions with varying meanings, and this creates differing systems of social events. It is not only that "good" or "bad" are differently defined: the actual empirical social happenings are also different.

Societies that are rapidly industrializing and urbanizing often exhibit extreme value clashes. New artifacts create new mechanics of social relations. Persons with relativistic and empathic stances thus for the first time gain institutional outlets that are consonant with and support their world-views. Traditional institutions still reinforce the old views, but the power of traditional leaders may well adjust and work through the new orderings. The result is often a mixture of old and new institutions, with old and new persons in each set. Value splits reflecting this intermingling then can appear within the class order. And so it comes to pass that admirals shoot admirals, generals shoot generals, labor-union members picket labor-union members, and law assumes so many meanings that the "habit of obedience" is eroded or lost. The consequent weakening of government makes either democratic or totalitarian solutions impossible, with feckless authoritarianism the remaining solution.

Developed nations suffer the same value ambivalences, although usually they show most clearly in foreign, not in domestic, affairs. The strength of national habit and custom, reinforced by national institutions and a common wash of primary education, usually prevents such value division from appearing in the country's domestic affairs. Still, many critics of American foreign policy contend that "moralism" directed outward is what has pushed the United States to fight total wars and demand unconditional surrenders, reinforcing absolutist perceptions now turning inward on domestic political processes.

Perhaps the best examples of value conflict are provided in the Latin culture world, where we find ornately complex and long-standing traditional structures, with remarkable powers of accommodation, alongside striking industrial and urban growth. The most advanced of the underdeveloped areas of the world, Iberia and Latin America reveal the widest range of types of human organization. Europe may stop at the Pyrenees and the Po, North America at the Rio Bravo, but what begins south of those lines? An abundant literature on the Latin "character" exists, making extended repetition unnecessary here. Whatever that character may be, there is good reason to think that many Italians, Spaniards, Portuguese, and Latin Americans see at least part of their lives in rationalistic, pragmatic, relativistic, and changeful ways. But certainly many of them are also firmly traditional in their values. A tenable hypothesis to explain the false starts, the hesitancies, and the zigzaggings in Latin development is that Latins no longer have a single, dominant way of looking at the world, heartily reinforced by the powers that be. Instead, there is enormous uncertainty concerning the uses of the instrumental institutions built in imitation of those in Protestant countries as well as in continuation and emendation of traditional Mediterranean society. If this hypothesis is valid, then we can begin to explain why elaborate educational institutions, great cities, complex communications systems, reasonably high standards of living, and complex industrial establishments are not guaranteed launching pads for "take-off" to self-sustaining political and social growth.

Argentina provides the most striking demonstration of a modern "infrastructure" that cannot by itself create an equally modern "superstructure." Almost nine out of ten Argentines are literate; by student enrollment the University of Buenos Aires is the largest in the Western Hemisphere (just a few years ago one out of every five Latin American university students was in an Argentine school); the country has the seventh-longest rail network in the world; in 1930 there were more automobiles per capita in Argentina than in either Great Britain or Sweden. Over seven million persons live in Buenos Aires, and a third of the national population is urban. Argentina is ethnically overwhelmingly European, including large German, English, and East European components resting on a "base" of Spanish and Italian immigrants. The climate is temperate, resources abundant, the scenery beautiful, and the food excellent and plentiful.

Since 1930 Argentina has passed through a series of military revolts, some classically liberal, but most of right-wing corporate persuasion. The lack of political continuity has been felt by its citizens in constant threats to their civil liberties, the disenfranchisement of masses of them, experiments with personality cults, extraordinarily cheap public ideologies, and other evidences of a loss of national way. Discussions about what is wrong with Argentina consume much cocktail-party time as well as enormous amounts of paper.

Part of the problem is almost certainly a matter of simple habit. "Revolutionary gymnastics," some Argentines call it. The men of the armed forces are by this time institutionalized plotters. They have convinced themselves that they have a special role in Argentine national life, and every time they quit office, the mess they leave behind is the start of a justification for further coups on the grounds of civilian ineffectiveness. Naturally, some civilians rapidly catch onto the game and join with military men in what many of them firmly believe to be a sacred mission. But how did the habit begin, and why is it that the schisms rend the middle and upper groups even more deeply than the lower ones?

The specific train of events began in 1930 with a typical

crisis of ideological identification, triggered by economic difficulties as well as by a "crisis of access," with urban working groups clamoring to be incorporated into Argentina's political, economic, and social status systems. One part of the middle and upper groups was in a democratic, liberal alliance. Another was dedicated to the politics of aristocracy, exclusionism, official Catholicism, and falangism. Neither saw the consequences of its stance: the former did not know how to build a national, participatory democratic structure, nor did it have the power and dedication to do so; the latter could not bring itself to the ruthless destruction of their class colleagues required for a truly totalitarian solution. In short, the democrats were not sufficiently democratic, the authoritarians not sufficiently repressive, and since neither side had sufficient insight to recognize the depths of the division between them, there was no way to achieve any meaningful politics of compromise or coalition. In the meantime, Argentina's skilled workers were socialists, communists, anarchists, or moderates allied with the Radicals who were in power from World War I to the Great Depression. Semiskilled workers and, later, the unskilled laborers coming to the cities from the countryside with the urban explosion of World War II tended to align with the radical conservative elements whose charismatic high point was marked by the Perón era (1945-55).

In short, the value-split cut the country vertically, putting all class segments into alignment on one or the other side of a massive dispute over what they considered proper for this life. Using the same language, institutions, streets, and national framework, the Argentines drifted into two different value worlds for all practical national purposes. The present government includes, in very high places, many persons who are unmistakably fascist; others are classical liberals. (The former cluster in the Ministries of the Interior, Education, and Religion; the latter are allowed to play with the economic agencies.) Except where daily life touches the formal governmental structure, it proceeds with a fair amount of freedom, dignity, and preservation of personal integrity. If the advantages of national community are little enjoyed, the disadvantages of an effectively repressive national community are also absent.

Argentina exemplifies the hypothesis that value-conflict engages all other levels of conflict. The multiple causes of the initial breakdown of 1930 have to do with *institutional factors*—the condition of the world market, Argentina's rural export and industrial import economy, wage distribution, labor organization, pressure groups, and so on; with *ideological and personal factors*—the presence of large numbers of recent Italian and Spanish immigrants, the ideological impact of Mussolini, Primo de Rivera, Salazar, and the then corporativist Church, the weakness of its capitalist and parliamentary ideological systems, personalism in political and other elements of social life, and so on; with the *existing power distribution*—the long-standing split between rural and urban elements, between Buenos Aires and the interior, the gap between immigrants and others, the way political power was centralized and yet spread through upper- and middle-class groups, and so on; and with *value factors:* traditionalist and modern views of the world, reinforced by overt ideologies, the educational system, and so forth. These elements—with many refinements that would be added in an analysis dedicated to this subject in itself—came together in such a way as to destroy any neat patterning of class-values-interest cohesion. Instead, class groups, family groups, interest groups, and others turned on themselves, to become fragmented from within. In such a situation, problems are judged not on the basis of the pragmatic possibilities inherent in given solutions, but rather on the basis of whether the available solutions are morally right or wrong. Thus, the area of rational choice is severely restricted, becoming instead the rationalization of absolute moralities in opposition. In this fashion, politics becomes primitive in a setting that otherwise seems "developed."

The Argentine experience is worth pondering, especially at a time when political upheavals in many parts of the industrialized world suggest that "tropical" politics may be spreading. The once comfortable belief that a great distance separates developed from undeveloped societies is beginning to disappear as it becomes evident that no polity is inherently immune from value conflict. Certainly the terms of political discourse in Latin America, Western Europe, and the United States are becoming disquietingly similar—and the language of politics is no mean clue to the content of disagreement. The strain between order and liberty is an old refrain in Latin politics: it is now a daily part of North American political talk, accompanied by the same political neuroses, the same head-shaking, and the same slogans. "There can be no freedom without order." "First we must see that the law is upheld, and then we can redress injustice." "Who wants order if there is no freedom?" "It is immoral to obey an unjust law." The debate is discomfiting not only because its issues have long since been thoroughly considered in political thought, but also because the protagonists are virtually unable to understand or even "hear" each other. The splits dividing hard-core left, hard-core right, and soft center are now so deep that even the routine, habitual aspects of public

life are subjected to conscious questioning and normative
evaluation. A fresh look about us is desirable, but it is
freighted with the risk that we shall each see such different
landscapes that a coherent national life will be difficult to re-
establish.

Value conflict, then, in generating differing social realities,
involves all other areas of human experience and calls into
question total modes of life. It is the kind of conflict most to
be avoided if the protagonists want to maintain their social
system, and it is also the kind of conflict that must be made
real and understandable for total revolution. Since it is likely
that every society contains individuals and groups who hold
very different basic values, it is clear that societies must have
systems that prevent value-conflict from emerging if there is
to be change without social breakdown.

Conflict over Community Definition; Race and Class Conflict

Values concern the nature of the universe; the make-up
and extent of one's community is also a matter of profound
contention although it need not call into question world-
views. The two kinds of conflict often appear together, but
they are theoretically separable and should be kept apart in
any discussion of a strategy of how to act in conflict situations.
Values concern the *kind* of community we live in; it is another kind of problem to fight over *who* inhabits the community.

Class conflict fits in this scheme not as the generator of all
conflict, but as a type of contention in defining the extent of
the community. The French Revolution, for example, is commonly described as the result of the middle classes seeking to
take power from upper groups or eventually to share it with

them. Racial conflict in the United States, to take another instance, has profound class elements mixed in it: the black people's low level of educational attainment, high rate of unemployment, and low power of consumption are marks of a class distinction. Much of the political distress in developing countries is due to the nations' inability effectively to decide just which groups will participate in what way. The shared nationalist drive may be xenophobic and patrioteering, but it also may attempt to forge a genuinely national community, a self-aware and self-recognizing body of citizenry acting within the political and other social institutions of the national society.

The enlargement of the community may be a simple agglutinative change—an enlargement that does not change the nature of community organization. Population increases are this kind of enlargement, of course; extending the franchise to women is another instance. One can also easily imagine social groups slowly being incorporated into the national community in an order going down the status scale. But if the enlargement implies a redistribution of power, and in a manner that puts into question the values of the superordinate groups, we then have a classical internal revolutionary situation. Presumably, however, democratic societies have created ideological and institutional mechanisms that permit community broadening as each claimant group fulfills, in effect, the conditions for membership. In this sense, then, a "crisis of access" such as the one the American Negro is passing through today is a very old-fashioned and ideologically unnecessary trauma. That a nineteenth-century crisis can occur in the late twentieth century within a fairly developed democratic structure is evidence of differing rates of development among various societal elements, of the susceptibility of all political systems to crises of self-identification, and of the potential for retrogression to more primitive political forms as well as for the continued realization of ideals.

The social extension of the United States has been called into question twice within the past forty years. The first time was in the 1930s, when the great economic distance separating farmers, laborers, and entrepreneurs disturbed market mechanisms to an extent that contributed heavily to the Great Depression. Industry's relative centralization and tight communications system permitted it to react rapidly in adjusting supply to demand; as prices fell, production was restricted in the attempt to bolster them. In contrast, decentralized and small farmers, seeing their unit prices drop, attempted to increase production to maintain their money income. Labor, many segments of it unorganized and all of it trammeled by the application of anti-trust laws and injunctions, was unable to bargain effectively. The issue was obvious: was powerlessness in the economic order going to suppress people to such an extent that many would be expelled from other institutions as well and some would never even have the chance to participate? The crisis was met by government intervention to equalize economic power. Farmers were given a system of guaranteed prices; labor was guaranteed its right to organize and thus to bargain collectively. Economic redress accomplished through political channels underscored the meaning of the "nation," the total community—an action easily justified on the basis of existing American ideology and involving no revolutionary change, even though the changes in juridical and institutional arrangements were real and significant. The solution was reached without a serious value conflict; it did, however, demand ideological, inter-institutional, and intra-institutional adjustments—that is, it involved all the lesser arenas of possible conflict.

The second massive crisis of America's community definition is the present racial issue. Certain groups in both black and white communities want to define this conflict as one of values; other factions see it as susceptible to the same level of solution as the crisis of the 1930s. The Supreme Court clearly has taken the latter view. By discarding the "separate but equal" rule in public education, the Court has said, in effect, that institutional separation violates the rights of individuals as members of the social nation who are *equal before the nation*. And in the post-1955 series of civil-rights decisions the judiciary has acted to effect a reasonable extension of existing social ethic and law. Supporters of this approach argue that the racial crisis can be solved by a quantitative expansion of access and a qualitatively purer adherence to constitutional norm.

Both Southern segregationists and the advocates of separate black nationalism would agree to the statement that this conflict involves fundamentally different kinds of human beings, and that perforce no resolution is possible within a common set of community parameters. There are many variants of the ways of looking at the problem, of course, but the minimum model needed to give structure to the conflict involves the pros and cons on the values side, the pros and cons on the community and institutional sides, and their corresponding cross-conflicts.

A good example of the elaborateness of the conflicts arising from these manifold levels of perception is the position of Jews in the racial situation today. This ethnic group's political views are for obvious reasons overwhelmingly libertarian, opposed to the ostracism of any group on racial grounds, and strongly in favor of equal opportunity in the institutional structure. The institutional fact of the matter is, however, that in the black ghetto Jewish merchants and landlords have been singled out for attack by their black clients, while some black intellectuals are violently rejecting their long-standing Jewish political champions. These events cause puzzled consternation among many Jewish civil libertarians. Some Jews fall back on a religiously inspired "chosen-people" defense—in its way a values argument—seeing their role as that of the inevitable scapegoat, cursed by their ability to understand the sickness of their oppressors. Others seek refuge in the simple defense of established interests. But the avowed attitudes and voting records of a majority of urban American Jews seem to show that the reasons for the blacks' rejection of them are being painfully considered, and they are attempting to turn the argument into yet another channel—into ideological disagreement. That is, the anti-Semitism of some black nationalists is interpreted as a "natural" reaction to exploitation and deprivation, which can be changed only by going ahead with the job of national incorporation and social betterment; in the meantime, steps should be taken to induce black leaders to formulate coherent ways of thinking about political action that will not alienate potential allies. But ideological rapport presupposes a common community and shared goals. For the committed revolutionary, this lowering of the level of conflict is unacceptable, at least in the present heated moment.

Students of voting behavior have been among the first to point out the aptly named "ethnic mosaic," a partial resolution of the United States' community fragmentation. The strength of religious and ethnic variables in explaining political preferences is an enduring part of the American electoral scene, since these continue to define urban neighborhoods and even some rural areas. "Hyphenated America" is related to "American America" by an entanglement of class, ethnic, and national ties that are an important part of the cultural flavor of this country, as well as of some of its more neurosis-inspiring traits. When the Hollywood infantry squad of World War II presses into the jungles of New Guinea, it is composed of an Italo-American, a Jewish-American, an Irish-American, a Polish-American, a Midwestern farm boy, a Texas sharpshooter, and an East Coast first lieutenant of impeccable White, Anglo-Saxon, Protestant background (even if played by an actor whose parents were born in Lithuania). State dinners to introduce foreign visitors to the American scene still include the same ethnic squad, now with the addition of an Afro-American.

Whatever the lingering romance of such chips in the social mosaic, pecking order goes hand in hand with ethnicity, and this perturbs the solution of national problems. The particular and the universal do not fit well when Polish neighborhoods are enemy territory to black home purchasers, and when college presidencies are filled with careful attention to personal "background." As centralization and decentralization are not mutually exclusive concepts, so the maturation of the United States as a national community will in part depend upon the success with which we reinforce the positive cultural aspects of ethnic diversity without damaging the several layers of secular community.

Ideological Conflict

Let us recall that we are using the term "ideology" in a special sense, referring only to articulated and politically relevant polemical thought.[4] Socialism, capitalism, Marxism, anarchism, and syndicalism are examples, but always in this narrow sense; insofar as socialists, capitalists, Marxists, anarchists, or syndicalists have broad sets of attitudes toward life, these "isms" may also remain in the category we have called value sets. To repeat, the reason for making this distinction is that it is desirable to construct a scheme that reflects the realities of a contradiction between ideology and value in the same person.

The utility of the category of ideological, as opposed to value, conflict may be demonstrated by considering briefly the now dying argument that the end of ideology is at hand. A product of the post-World War II disillusionment with Marxist and Central European authoritarian ideologies, the "end of ideology" is a belief that in the present era we are repudiating grandly Messianic schemes, beginning a more reasonable pragmatic politics, not in defiance of the "system" and its works, but, rather, by seeking new distributions within extant patterns of social design. In the light of our present discussion we would analyze this argument as giving rise to two possibilities: ideology is withering because conflict has moved either to more profound levels or to more superficial ones. If the causes of the ruction stem from the mysteries of world-view or the agonies of defining one's social world, then the rationalizations of formal systems of explanation become secondary and often rapidly passing concerns; the left and the right and the good and the bad and the modern and the traditional may join in a united front of territorial and community defense. Or, the relativist and the absolutist may

---

[4] "A verbalized (or verbalizable), polemical set of ideas concerning the meaning of life in past, present, and future manifestations." Here I am dealing only with verbalized ideologies.

come to a parting of the ways, no longer able to share in community, institution, or any other affiliation. Unity for the defense of community is fairly common; a values schism is rarer, as we have said. In any event, both types of conflict can persist without extended formalizations of their reasons for being. In fact, the discord is usually so sharp and rapid as to preclude reasoning.

Ideology also weakens for an opposite reason, when it is no longer needed to guide conduct in low-level conflicts which have safely routinized procedures for settlement. In the United States, for example, the widely accepted myths of equality, classlessness, the American way of life, and so forth, tend to reduce *all* divisions, not merely those that come from differing systems of explanation. The appearance of value conflicts and community conflicts, however, has brought with it a thirst for formalized bodies of doctrine, whether domestic, like that of the John Birch Society, or partially imported, in the way Frantz Fanon has been for the black nationalists and Herbert Marcuse for the New Left. And the ideologies are used either as expendable tools by those who would like to deepen controversy, or as towering defenses by those who would like to prevent further or more intense dispute.

Again, then, we have another demonstration of the utility of arguing that higher levels of conflict tend to involve all lower levels. The converse is clearly not so, for otherwise we would have no way to explain such contained disagreements as strikes, elections, lawsuits, or even that ideological disputation disparagingly referred to as "coffeehouse talk."

Conflicts of Interest among Institutions

The usual way of thinking about social strife is as a clash between institutionally vested interests. That is, the routine materialistic interpretation of conflict presumes that it involves the defense of interests tied to a specific institution and satisfying specialized wants and needs—goods and services, desires for education, types of worship, the power of parents over children, and so on. "Interest" has so far been persistently, and implicitly, identified with perception: an "interest" is any perceived want, a desire, an opinion about something, with due regard for the depth of the opinion and the means available to individuals or groups to apply power to achieve satisfaction of that want. With this category, however, we move to more standard forms of analysis in which interests are not merely subjective (perceived), but objective (necessary to sustain individual and social life, whether so perceived or not), an approach consistent with the previous discussion of causality. This distinction between objective and subjective interests leads back once more to the need for discriminating between the universal and the particular. Objective interests are universal: if man is by nature gregarious, he needs institutional arrangements and ideas that permit him to live in some kind of community, whatever it may be; if he is to survive, he has to have food, shelter, clothing, and mates, whatever the cuisine, architectural style, fashion, or mating system may be. The concept of "culture" as used by anthropologists is useful here, as defining the range of subjective interests that set the conceptual limits for the objective ones.

As I pointed out in my earlier postulation of social class

as raw power potential, the working out of interests as well as of power involves habituations, accepted routines of behavior surrounding the satisfaction of given combinations of interests, or, to repeat, institutions. Because all institutions are culturally specific, with respect to institutional conflict I propose again to discard considerations of objective or universal interests, not only in order to shorten the analysis, but also specifically to turn away from the unexamined premise of conventional wisdom that man must in the first place satisfy his belly-needs before he can gratify his other wants. If that were so, in the hierarchy of interest the economic institution would come first. Now, that priority may well evidence itself among aware adults in times of extreme deprivation, but in any normal situation, including "average" poverty, good grounds exist for believing that familial, religious, and socialization procedures are cause for more profound concern than economic ones. It is not that satisfying material wants is not important, but rather that specific procedures used in economic matters are probably less important to people than how they behave and expect others to behave with reference to certain non-economic matters. Thus in most societies it may well be easier to change economic practices than family ones, for example.

The inference I am developing is that there is a hierarchy of significance attached to institutional performance that affects the nature of institutional conflict and the culturally conditioned definition of interest. The major institutions of the family, religion, education, the economy, and the polity can be listed in that order because in most societies that is the route through which humans become social human beings. Of course, there are individual differences. Some children, especially in secular societies, are surrendered to school before church. In periods of early industrialization, poor children may be given over to jobs without any chance of formal education at all. Whatever the order of exposure, however, I suggest that the earlier in life persons take on institutional roles, the more they tend to continue to view their place in such institutions as being whole, all-of-a-piece, an organic all-embracing unity. The infant has no choice but to begin to see the world through those immediately around him and to perceive it as a seamless web, and he only slowly singles out his institutional roles as he learns to participate in his society. He may continue to view the world as blob, in essentially infantile fashion; or he may learn to rationalize and analyze his world into distinguishable if not actually separate parts; or he may learn to accommodate a high degree of analytical rationalization with a yet higher order of synthesis. But he will probably always tend to see the family as more integral and universal an occurrence than the economy or the educational system. The importance of individual variation in these perceptions is clear, particularly so when the range of acceptable styles of institutional behavior is broad. In any event, it is enough for our purposes here to postulate that people's persistence in holding on to their individual views of institutions produces a hierarchy of intensities and attitudes concerning them.

In modern or modernizing societies—including the maliciously titled "overdeveloped" societies like the United States—the institution of politics is probably the focus of greatest perceptual conflict. The institution of the modern state is a focus for disagreements concerning the proper spheres and ordering of other institutions. The function of the national state is to synthesize, to be the ultimate arbiter of the disagreements spawned within and among the other institutional structures. Family, religion, education, and the economy operate analytically, in that they describe specific activities and functions, often given further definition by age and generational particularity. But the special function of modern politics is generalization—an overarching adjudication mechanism that synthesizes control. This is not true in pre-modern societies, where political, religious, and other functions are often institutionally mingled. But the modern situation presumes a national community (the nation-state) as the locus of familial, economic, educational, and social development. Political discord thus is more liable to explode into normative and community conflict than other institutional conflicts not involving a direct relationship to the definition of state power. It may be further ventured that the more organic the feelings about any institution, the more bitter and resistant to solution will be any conflict between it and the state.

A truism of political theory today is that, as modernization proceeds, institutional differentiation and functional specificity grow—indeed, that this very growth comprises the modernization process itself. Institutional differentiation makes specialization possible; functional specificity describes its limits; both are conditions for the efficiency of industrial society. As it stands, the argument is important and unexceptional, and I mention it again here because it is only through *conflict* that delimitations of sphere and function are set firmly enough to be accepted as norms as the modernization process develops, and these resolutions can be reached and maintained only if there is an appropriate political apparatus. The separation of church and state, for example, has been one of the most difficult of institutional divorces to achieve in the presently modern world. The enormous violence attending religious conflict is known to anyone who is even superficially acquainted with European history, and present-day events prove that the matter has not been wholly laid to rest. Whether the state should provide textbooks for parochial-school students is still an issue in the United States, converted since the Korean War into "one nation under God." The function of the religious institution in the Islamic world is still undefined and a source of constant difficulty as Muslim nations try to modernize. The birth-control issue and the position of the Catholic Church on it is a conflict that perturbs more than just the Mediterranean culture world. The separation of church from state is not merely a device to set the necessarily absolutist aside from what one hopes is the limited; it also can go far toward creating a no-man's land, a neutral strip, in what is always a potentially frightful battleground.

The legislation of morality and family relations, too, is always a difficult area for state action. Although governments attempt it, the short-term result is usually one of violence and coercion, for the family is usually the institution most resistant to political manipulation. When police states recruit people to denounce members of their own family, the sense of outrage created is not a simple political response, but often a cry out of the individual's personal security system. The Chinese Communist government has gone far in breaking extended kin relations and superimposing its new hierarchy of institutional loyalties on Chinese culture, but it is finding it very hard going in the core of family life. Politics can certainly affect families, but great power is needed, and its application must be microcosmic—fine and detailed—and at the same time ruthlessly firm.

We can all think of many other instances of inter-institutional conflict. We should notice that they can be broken into two major categories: those involving ideologies, community definition, and values—the higher orders of conflict; and those restricted to the institutional system itself. It is in the latter category, by and large, that we find distributional conflicts: farmers fighting to maintain the price levels of their commodities consonant with the cost of industrial products, labor arguing with management, or consumers (these could be farmers, industrialists, or laborers) protecting consumer interests often against themselves in other organizational roles.

Conflicts of Interest within Institutions

This type of conflict is at the lowest level we shall consider here. The most frequently observable of conflict situations, it is, in its cumulative effect, fully as significant as the others. Its nature concerns the issue of how deprivations and rewards, fairly narrowly defined, are distributed. Who gets what positions? Which bills are reported out by what congressional committees? What textbook will be used to teach beginning reading? Should Company A merge with Company X or Y? The history of the settlement of such disputes sets the tone for a total institution, for the decisions taken are the little steps which, cumulatively, tell us whether change is possible within the institution or whether it must be imposed from outside, thereby incurring other types of conflict.

Small cumulative settlements, and the limited yet additive rewards of the gains and losses they apportion, have large consequences in that they help to set the terms not only for society-wide change, but also for individual and group mobility. Institutions are the foci of personality, class, and norms, for it is through overt behavior that pay-off is measured, whether by actor or observer. In turn, what one does in an institutional setting can affect one's class position, condition one's avowed attitudes, and tone one's temperament. Institutions are the scene of alienation and accommodation, of striving, of defeat and success, and where power or weakness is evidenced. These manifestations work themselves out in two classically accepted ways: interaction among the guardians of each institution, and between the guardians and the institution's public users. Clash and cooperation among guardians, or bureaucrats, are the stuff of public administration, small-group analysis, and daily newspapers. Much less structured in formal social thought and analysis is the play between officials and laymen.

I have already commented upon the relationship between personal mobility within an institution and the resulting, personally held power transferable from generation to generation. In brief recapitulation, we might mention such cases as pharmacists who become presidential aspirants by rising through the political institution, or celebrities whose luster comes from a combination of salary and status. Even the small differences in income between white-collar and skilled blue-collar workers in most countries can hide very real power differences. The basic distinction between the two groups is not in the amount they are paid, or in the prestige advantage of clean and soft hands over grimy and callused ones. It stems from the difference in the daily exercise of power by each one. A low-paid postal employee can snarl at and bully hundreds of people every day, use some of the weight of the government to make others respond to his arbitrariness, and work out his personal frustrations on strangers with relative impunity. A blue-collar worker is largely denied the use of such power, being at the tag end of the hierarchy and more or less without institutional levers he can use in this daily fashion, with the possible exception of his trade union if he belongs to one. Salary is not the determinant here. One may say the white-collar employee is enjoying psychic income, but it would be more direct and less falsely allusive of economic motivation to say that he is certifying a real institutional difference on a constant, day-to-day basis.

The formal structures of institutions are the means through which authorities work their influence, whether they be parents rearing their children, or heads of state guiding their citizenry. Naturally, there is a seeping away of power in all directions. At the highest political levels, for example, an obvious loss of authority occurs when chief executive officers are hampered by military commanders or recalcitrant religious leaders, or by economic chiefs who sabotage their work by means of legal loopholes, lockouts, and slowdown strikes. Even unanimity at the top of the institutional authority does not guarantee that the trickle through the apparatus to the subject can always occur without drastic change. In the nature of the situation, no formal member of the institutional structure is without some measure of power. Thus a clash within the institution may range bureaucratic followers against bureaucratic leaders in virtual open revolt. Schoolteachers who oppose the rulings of a school board, policemen whose association countermands a mayor's orders, and party members who bolt party tickets are acting out what we mean when we say "institutional breakdown." These occurrences introduce a note of confidence-shattering unpredictability and carry with them the danger of touching off much more intensive and extreme discord.

Even when institutions are firm and strong, friction between the functionary and the user often develops to the point where we can use the word "alienated" as descriptive of the latter's attitude, including by that term any feeling that the social institutions are unresponsive to individual style and preference. Whatever the ideological or stylistic intent of the institution's leaders, the possibility of alienation always exists when those who apply institutional *diktats* in personal situations are wooden and autocratic. They can help to set a tone in daily life that rasps against feelings to a degree where reason departs and direct action takes over. If "whitey" persists in making the black man invisible, then at least one way to become visible is to bump into whitey on the street. Of such small irritations can grand movements grow. It is not that it is historically "necessary" that intra-institutional conflict get out of hand, but it can and does.

It is worth emphasizing that customary behavior and the pursuit of specific interests can serve to cover over latent value differences. Even colleagues who understand the deeper meanings of their roles in different ways and who define their actions in conflicting senses can continue at more superficial levels to work together so long as ultimate interests are not called into active question. Latency is an important condition here, infusing a sense of social time into the processes of collective action. Latency and unevenness of perceptions in conflict situations combine to introduce the next part of this discussion, the matter of asymmetry in the means-and-ends views of actors in clash.

The Confrontation with the Enemy

This conceptually linked listing, or typology, of conflict just presented should not be taken at face value as being descriptively true of reality. There is no need to commit the nominalist fallacy that to name is to create. The list is merely a proposed way of thinking about certain social matters, and whether it is any good or not depends on its power to help us diagnose and predict. But the list also has ideological color. It assumes many things: that social events can be rationally studied (many deny this, or would not have it done even if they believed it); that conflict in itself is a tactically useful area of study; that no social happenings can be adequately examined on the basis of single-cause and lineal analysis; and that human "contradiction" is more often in the eye of the scientific beholder than of the social actor. These assumptions and others define reality, contribute to making reality, and yet are not the all of reality. They are not mere opinion, but artifacts for the organization of data, subject to testing.

Let us talk first of conflict and individual integrity, and then about the definition of the "enemy" in "conflict situations." Both issues exercise the liberal conscience, and the second is implied in much of political thought since Machiavelli.

Political and religious rhetoric often tells us that we should be "true to ourselves," integral men and women with the courage to let our innermost beings shine through in our relations with our fellows. More dangerously, we are told to act in accordance with our most profound convictions because only thus can we be truly honest. But our good sense tells us the world would be a jungle were we to obey these injunctions. The "state of nature" beloved of early English political theorists is not idyllic, but one in which political man lets his values guide his right arm. Let us consider the elements of politics discussed in Chapter I, and add them to the typology discussed in this chapter, and ask what would happen if the filters were removed between man the socialized being in a complex world and man the integral being acting out his basic normative views in all situations.

We can start by presuming that all men have some individual characteristics: some of us are ritualistic and organicist, some rationalist and relativist; some of us are stupid and insensitive, some intelligent and sensitive; some of us suffer only for and in ourselves, others suffer as well for their fellows. I need not belabor the point that social life would grind to a disagreeable halt if we had to try to live with behavior that reflected only who the actor was or how he felt, without regard to what kind of action might best fit a given situation. Why should an organicist stop for a traffic light if he believes his government's taxation policy is unjust? Why should not an absolutist gun a man down if he has defined him out of the human race on ethnic, ideological, or other grounds entirely reasonable in the mind of this man, who is sure he knows and reflects universal truth, indeed, who believes that if he did not act to remove the anti-Christ he would suffer damnation? It is clear that socially we can afford to be true to ourselves only if that truth is a generous and honest decency.

The obvious point having been made, what are the consequences of making it? One conclusion is that consistency is not only the balm of the small-minded, but also the poison of social order. The major premise of *civis* is that men should be kept from interacting on the basis of their primary belief-systems and, instead, should be kept acting on the basis of routine and of secondary belief-systems—at the least, aphorisms learned in school; at the most, consciously formulated and intellectually verifiable ideologies. A sound polity will hold dispute to the intra-institutional level. Conflicts *between institutions* are part of the normal adjustments to change, but they can lead to rather superficial revolutions that do not accomplish enough to be worth while, especially in countries in the early stages of industrial growth. Ideological dispute is more dangerous, for it is a simulacrum of value conflict, and invites a crusade's bloodshed and dedication. Discord concerning community identity and organization is even riskier, for it mobilizes institutions, classes, and ideological systems into battle against other institutions, classes, and ideological systems. Value-conflict spells the end of a single polity, leading to divorce or death, not permitting compromise unless the level of conflict is lowered.

Because every dispute can be made to travel the road to ultimate schism, system-maintenance requires that conflict be kept to as low a level as possible. The only way to do so without coercion, which in itself may deepen conflict, is through a full recognition of individual and group differences, a recognition served by institutional separatenesss. This containment of dispute, at least, is what the modern society is structurally better able to do than the traditional or primitive society. There is nothing paradoxical, then, about concluding that the best way to permit individuals to continue to cherish their most profound differences is to inhibit the effective expression of those differences in their over-all social behavior. The best way a Muslim living in New York can continue to believe that killing an infidel is a passport to heaven is by not acting on the belief.

A second inference from the premise that to be stubbornly and consistently integral in thought and behavior is socially damaging is that the proper performance of various institutional roles requires various appropriate *and differing* ways of knowing and acting. Some ways of knowing proceed from faith, or aesthetic insight and taste. Others are biologically stimulated and conditioned. Still others are evidential and testable, limited in extension—in short, scientific knowledge. These ways of knowing and of valuing are not distributed evenly among individuals, nor throughout all institutions, nor among various age groups. Cretins cannot "know" in the same way as geniuses. Religious and aesthetic "knowledge" cannot be validated by scientific methods. "Knowing" that one is hungry or that one feels enclosed and stifled differs from "knowing" that one should have taken a finesse in bridge. The various modes of acquiring and accumulating knowledge require differing validity tests and thus differing kinds of normative support. That is, the moral justification for acting in a given way depends upon the kind of knowing legitimately required for that specific family of behavior. A violinist's sense of the music's style and period may prompt him to adopt tempi that a critic may condemn on aesthetic grounds, but certainly the critic will not apply moral criteria, for aesthetic norms need not carry moral overtones. Age alone contributes to differences in the meaning of "knowing." As Jean Piaget has pointed out so forcibly, children's thought processes are pre-rational (not irrational) and their perceptions are keyed to synthesize and integrate in their search to define the wholeness of their being.

The completely civilized man, then, is one able to differentiate both among his institutional roles and among his normative sets with respect to those roles. That is to say, he is the ultimate relativist because he sees the importance of absolute convictions in certain areas and relative convictions in others; he is the ultimate rationalist because he perceives the necessity (not merely the desirability) of non-rational behavior in certain spheres of conduct as well as at certain stages in the life cycle. And he is the ultimately changeful man, because he understands when he must not move as well as when he must.

The essential rule here would seem to be that the more personally individual the behavior (because of age, faith, and biological and stylistic factors of judgment), the more holistic must be the supporting values. The more social a manifestation (the more interaction with other humans across dividing lines of class, temperament, and varied role), the more it requires a relativistic value structure. I therefore conclude that to be true to oneself, a person should be integral only with respect to the roles he is playing at any given time and in the way appropriate to these roles. To be true to other people, and for others to be true to him, he should exercise—and be allowed to exercise—the values and behavior appropriate to and supportive of the pertinent behavior. The reward of the complexity of modern life is that the modern individual is permitted, even required, to be many individuals. A reversion to wholeness in the sense of a seamless singularity of personal characteristics, behavior, and values is a retrogressive cultural and personal impoverishment.

This discussion is directly relevant to problems of political tactics, for it sets the stage for a consideration of the kinds of antagonists that can be found in conflict situations. Although nothing could be plainer than that we need to know the nature of the enemy if we are to be efficacious politically, learning what that nature is and deciding how to act are not easy in practice, if only because of inhibitions bred by the intellectual sensitivity, ideological stance, and value commitments through which interests are felt and defined. A man profoundly committed to legal process may find himself confronted by a universal dogmatist who will use any means in pursuit of his ends. Or, the guardians of law may engage in illegal activity. What is a democrat to do in such cases? Such questions are the usual ones raised in moments of great national crisis, when civil disobedience becomes attractive for many dissidents. There can be no definitive guide to conduct in matters so closely related to social ethics, but perhaps we can propose diagnostic tools for their evaluation.

The conflict typology I have presented here permits the possibility of an asymmetrical clash of a kind which so far we have not discussed: that is, we have not considered clashes in which one group acts as though absolutely basic world-views were at issue, while others think a more superficial disagreement is involved. It is easy to see that the more traditionalist a party to a dispute, the more will that party tend to deepen the level of conflict, to presume that God and morality and the parking ticket are all as one; the more differentiated or modern a mentality, the more it will tend to keep the dispute at levels of possible compromise. The analytical prickliness of the matter enters when these differing perceptions mingle in the same conflict situation. Then mutual understanding becomes difficult, the discovery of common procedures for negotiation tends to take forever, and in extreme cases compromise is impossible. Such asynchronous conflict is an extremely common occurrence. How many times have we heard the cool ones accuse the others of "overreacting"? How many times have we heard someone defend a point on principle, while others argue for a pragmatic ("opportunistic," according to the opposition) solution? Finding a "proper" level at which to contain conflict and defining the level are preconditions to successful conflict resolution.

The traditionalist's advantage is his certitude of moral rightness, the essential simplicity and absoluteness of his conviction. His disadvantage is that he finds it difficult to understand his opponent's views, and he is rigid in strategy if not tactics. The relativist's advantage is that he can understand the mind of the traditionalist and be tactically agile. His disadvantage is that his very empathy tends to stay his hand, makes him believe that the conflict can somehow be compromised, and makes it difficult for him to believe that there are enemies who under certain conditions cannot be assuaged. The organicist lives in devotion to the principle that his enemies ought to be totally defeated. The relativist tries to avoid the recognition that there are times when the toleration of absolutism is incompatible with the survival of his own alternative.

Two of the great landmarks of modern political thought offer solutions to the problem of how to reconcile violent action with the due processes of an open and secular society. Developed, fittingly, in the early period of the secular nation-state, the first addresses itself to the right of the citizen to deny ultimate power to the governor. Locke and Hobbes, in their natural law theories, laid the basis for withdrawing tacit consent from the state when political leaders use public power to deprive persons of their "natural rights." The importance of such thinking lies not in whether the concept of natural law is logically consistent, but rather in the more mundane political purpose of establishing a rational basis for disobedience, and ultimately for revolution. The other doctrine, coming late in the development of the nation-state, concerns the use of law to protect the state against a dissident citizenry. Best expressed in the "clear and present danger" decisions of the United States Supreme Court, the argument, simply put, is that normal constitutional guarantees of procedure and also of certain substantive elements can be set aside when there is an evident risk that the exercise of individual rights can lead to immediate and irreparable hurt. The first doctrine prescribes the permissible extreme individual action, the second the permissible extreme state action.

Both doctrines can be dangerous in practice. Loose definitions of individual rights may get in the way of concerted action just when it is most needed; loose definitions of the imminence of danger may open the way to authoritarianism robed as democracy. The second risk is the greater, of course, as a simple matter of practical community consensus politics. The two doctrines are useful reminders, however, that a base has been laid for thinking in terms of boundary lines that separate actions contained within law from those that may *legitimately* be taken outside the normal legal and institutional structures and practices. As conceptual artifacts of democratic systems, the two doctrines tell relativists, whether citizens or public officials, when they must become absolutist.

Manifestations of these matters are extraordinarily varied. The appropriate response of a German democrat to nazism is easy to figure from a distance, but rather difficult inside the situation. The proper stance of a relativistic Soviet scientist to his country's dogmatic political system is not simply and comfortably determined. Or again, how much should the traditional political tool of personalism be used by a modernist leader who seeks democratic ends for an underdeveloped society?

The truly relativistic political man risks grave civic error if he fails to understand that there may come a time when it is imperative to read his opponent out of the game. So long as prevailing institutional rules and procedures are open and pragmatic, and are inclusive of and acceptable to a broadly based citizenry, and so long as the persons attached to the dogmatic opposition behave by the rules, then the only unpleasantness stems from the bargaining process itself. But all situations are mixed, and even in democratic countries certain institutions and certain leadership and follower groups maintain citadels of intransigent and mystical irrationality. The democrat should recognize the danger of such rigidity, especially in the public sphere, and should be ready to acknowledge that there are times when substantive relief may not be possible. If the matter concerns institutional or system continuity or physical survival, he should recognize when he has been pushed to *his* limit, pressed back on his own basic value commitment. He should then act out of the same sense of conviction and the same determination that motivates his opponents, albeit with regret for the enormous loss implied in the breakdown of impersonal law. The conflicts may be minor, with little resonance, such as disagreement among faculty members, or they may be of some magnitude, such as those of racial discrimination. But in all cases the believer in the value of public freedom should understand that the range of possible solutions has not been exhausted when all the available laws and regulations and other procedures have been gone through. He must also understand the hierarchy of conflict and recognize when the failure has been one of level of discourse, understanding, and interest. An inability to act with a decisiveness appropriate to the level of antagonism has brought shame to many a liberal and his cause. The liberal's fallacy is to think that even the commitment to liberalism is relative; this condemns him to be victimized by the dogmatists. (The fake liberal, however, is one who thinks that the *application* of his relative commitment is absolute.)

Generous men prefer not to believe that some political men are implacable enemies of freedom. But in a world so heavily peopled with totalitarians ready for violence and with comfortable hypocrites who genteelly exclude others from equality of opportunity, a libertarian politics requires a clear understanding of what an adequate response to conflict is. The dogmatic enemy should not be fought with the same weapons or the same sanctions he uses, nor should he be fought equally on all fronts. The outlines of a strategy of conflict-understanding for the libertarian in democratic countries might be as follows:

—He should try to make access to conflict-resolution procedures open to all and strive to make them easy and understandable.

—He should try to keep public rules and regulations and their application as flexible as possible.

—He should not enter into ideological and value disagreements if solutions to conflicts are reasonably well respected by all the parties concerned.

—He should try to restrict public disagreement to public matters, steering away from intimate and highly charged questions of religious belief and family affairs except when a clear public interest is involved, as in education.

—He should recognize the intellectual and emotional

difficulties of his absolutist opponents not in order to respect or emulate them, but in order to understand their full danger and to contain them within the play of customary behavior as far as possible.

—He should respect procedures for maintaining law and order in their full extension and exhaust all their remedies before taking unlawful action.

—He should be prepared for limited unlawful action when it is reasonable to believe that his society is ready for or urgently needs to extend the libertarian order to promote participation in existing institutions and the rational settlement of public problems, and when no other ways are open and the only alternative is a continued and significant loss of liberty.

—In extreme cases he should recognize that no compromise solutions are immediately possible, and act on that recognition in whatever ways will least damage the ability to reconstruct a decent order. His only effective choices in this situation are emigration, sabotage, or overt violence; the non-effective ones are silence or suicide.

—In sum, he should remember that a truly libertarian man must be rational as long as he can, but always admit that his belief in rationality is at base a dogma, and thus respect his own ultimate sticking point.

The point of no return can now be spelled out. When there is no public space in which to be reasonable and rational, the rational man will recognize that he must abandon due process. That room for maneuver is gone when institutions collapse in upon themselves, when all categories of knowledge and all justifications become one, when society becomes an institutional, normative, and cognitive monolith. Long before that pure state of totalitarianism approaches, the pursuer of freedom will recognize the danger. He then must choose either to make a number of distasteful responses of alliance and power creation and action, or to remove himself if he can. Above all, in the early stages of decay he must fight its evidences: children should not be brought into the world for the glory of the nation-state; God should not be used as a lackey of politics; education should not be used to freeze minds into stultified obedience to public or other authority; the economy should not be glorified as a sacred artifact constructed in heaven for the aggrandizement of some of the people; and the state and its temporary manipulators should, in the discharge of their difficult functions, be received with skeptical acceptance but never adulation. *Always* ask what it is proper for your state to do for you, and *never* ask blindly what it is that you can do for your state. The old lessons of the separation of powers and of a contained government under law are forgotten only at great risk to democracy. Nor should that other, more esoteric lesson be neglected: when symptoms become apparent, the disease may be too far gone for cure. Liberal politics demands constant attention if we are to move from an imperfect democratic order to a less imperfect one. To stand still is to go backward, and it is crucial to attend to the alienated and the exiled, for they are a never-ceasing test of public honesty.

Though the pacifist will protest mightily, I submit that under certain conditions there is no alternative but to break laws and be aggressive in the defense of better social ways against worse ones. I propose the legitimacy of illegality only in extreme cases, however, and only as last resort against regression into increasing authoritarianism. The pacifist's philosophical stance rests on the Stoic idea that all men share a common humanity and that to kill is to become as bad as the aggressor against whom one defends oneself. I do not share these ideas. On the contrary, I assert that in social matters some men are qualitatively different from others and that this qualitative difference sometimes appears stark naked in the political process. I also contend that not all killers are alike, any more than all housewives are the same, or all social events. Just as being modern in one sphere does not mean that one is modern in others, so killing for certain reasons is not the same as killing for other reasons, nor does the fact of killing for certain reasons mean that the killer will also kill for other reasons. If relativism has any social validity, it is possible and even necessary to be relativistic about death.

The clearest sign that a political system is working badly is an outburst of extreme action. Police killing looters or snipers killing police, mob violence and its accompaniments, are evidence that new powers and ideas exist that have no ready channels for expression. The creation of such channels is a basic reason for the existence of any responsive and open political order. When the channels are not created, we must conclude that the government is not acting for all its citizens but, instead, is defending specific as opposed to national community interests. In a partially democratic society such defalcation blends "legal" into "illegal" violence by depriving legality of broad consensual acceptance and imbuing illegality with ethical legitimacy. Angry cops who break laws as well as heads are sometimes applauded. The problem is as old as bad politics.

Conclusions and Recapitulation

At this point, the major propositions of this book have been laid down. It remains to apply them—and to denote the non-testable ideological commitments that underlie them. But first let us briefly summarize the argument.

To begin, the time spans with which we are concerned range from short to long but do not include the entire sweep of human history or the rise and fall of civilizations. I have tried to exclude long-run deterministic analysis from the discussion in order to push explanation as far as possible within empirically testable propositions, and without recourse to universal principles.

These chronological and theoretical limitations demand that causality be treated as a historical occurrence only; that is, I have sought to explain cause in terms of how historically bounded cultural variation is affected, not in terms of how the general course of human development is affected. The result is to see causality as incorporating some measure of autonomy in decisions to act, without rejecting the significance of "mindless" and conditioned responses to physical environment, external occurrences, and the facts of internal social organization. Consequently, within the historical limits I have set, I see cause as containing the possibility for effective action, and the causal process as differing qualitatively by the degree to which human intervention in the processes of change involves the exercise of reason or of customary reaction.

The elements to take into account in assessing a society's ability to act are: the reservoirs of different persons that can be drawn on for more or less effective action; the ways in which individuals imbue their situations with social meaning; the institutions available to express decision; and the intellectual, empathetic, and ideological capacities of actors in both leadership and follower positions.

While these elements are necessary to understand social change, they are not sufficient. Sufficiency of explanation is achieved only in the configurations into which the elements fall by habit or are consciously placed. Conscious decision on significant matters can be effective in theory because the correlations among class, values, institutions, and personality are not universal but, rather, historical and culture-bound. In traditional societies, with little institutional differentiation or role specialization, we find consistency of correlation among the elements of political analysis. The more developed a society, the less consistency we find, and the clearer it is that class position only very vaguely indicates value set, that the two together poorly predict institutionalized behavior, and that the three together will be a weak indicator of personal variation within roles and statuses. (These may, however, have greater usefulness in considering a society that emphasizes class divisions and uniformity of behavior within class groups.) No matter what the order in which we mix the elements, the correlations will be of only shadowy utility or will fail in comparative analyses.

Because each element is itself a complex variable, we should also expect that, with modern complexity, asymmetries will grow within each measure. Economic, social, and political power are never to be found in balance in a rapidly changing situation, nor, for that matter, in all static ones. Value postures are usually not the same with regard to the family as they are to the economy. Human behavior changes in style and content in accord with age, sex, and institutional area. Competence and empathy need not go hand in hand; nor need ideological rationalizations fit values or other personality elements. Naturally, the particles will form patterns everywhere, but I emphasize again that certain configurations can be striking in one culture without implying similar strength of combination in others. We must be wary of finding the universal in culture-limited evidence.

The theoretical and methodological implications of this view are that we should be wary of theories with an implicit tendency to emphasize evenness and rationality; that we need theories which discriminate general happenings from historically significant clusterings of events, so that we can make valid intercultural comparisons; and that we must find methods that do not flatten interacting differences into insignificant likenesses.

The ideological consequence of this view is that we are pushed to a full consideration of where reason and will take their places in political action and change. Breaking down deterministic connections among structural, normative, and behavioral elements invites us to consider the range of effective choice open within varying dimensions of interacting possibilities, freeing us from thinking of change as but oscillation about a single line.

▪▪▪ Communities and Commitments

*On time, taxonomy, and the institutional
orders of pluralism in democracies and
corporate states, and a discussion of
public and private interest*

Clock time measures unchanging units; social time measures
the relationship between clock time and degrees of social
change. Clock time records identical, repetitive operations
whose continuance does not carry in itself any seeds of explanation; social time refers to process, never precisely repetitive, the understanding of which is twined into the on-
going happenings themselves. Social expressions such as
"long term" and "short term" do not refer directly to clock
time, for they are estimations of the ratio between social
time and clock time.

Time has been an explicit ingredient in the thesis of this
book. The chronological time spans have been held to incidents, decades, or at most a century in the life of a society.
The social time spans have also been constrained, falling
short of the life careers of cultures. The persistent thesis
has been that, in *particular and temporally fairly short social processes,* the connections that might appear logical to a
social scientist seeking consistency tend to break down. I
have considered these chinks as inspiring optimism, for when-

ever we can demonstrate that consequences are not determined by *a priori* factors such as class, culturally defined interest, or accidents of personality, we are also implying that human will is a part of the causal complex. This thesis is good only in specific and limited cases, however, and of course carries the cargo of a value judgment. Nevertheless, we can use the elements of political life already discussed so as to cast light on social time in limited clock-time periods. Let us attempt that exercise first, in the expectation that we shall still be left wondering about the grand events of human history: the emergence of industrial civilization; or monotheism, and Islam, Judaism, and Christianity; or the medieval world and its relation to the Renaissance.

The political elements outlined in Chapter I and combined in Chapter II come into view once again, this time as variables in terms of this degree of temporal compression in any given social event. Let us hypothesize that, in a stable situation in which value, class, or institutional conflicts are absent, an election will revolve about the one variable left—the candidates' personal characteristics. Now, an election is a point-in-time occurrence and thus is a logical focus for emphasizing the candidates' personalities, ideologies, and competence, even when other arenas of clash are open. So, if the clock-time span is very short, or the social-time span uncluttered, we may expect the most easily affected variable, personal characteristics, to come to the fore.

Social-time speeds as institutional and class factors become involved, but the rate can be measured only by equating the passage of chronological time with the intensity and spread of the institutional and class changes. The industrial "revolution" is given that name only because economies, other institutional structures, and eventually class composition changed in certain countries within what was considered a very short period. Many Latin American "revolutions," on the contrary, are not given that name, despite the use of violence in changing political leadership, because the consequence is often merely a change in personnel, with no substantial modification of the political system or its bureaucracy.

This approach to social time is little more than an explicit recognition of what scholars and ordinary men usually take for granted. Studies of an election commonly focus on individuals, accidents, anecdotes, and public reactions to them. Studies of a government administration or regime tend to be about policies, institutional adjustments, laws, and the part individuals play in the changes. Studies of periods of national history assume that an even broader base is necessary, and bring in social movements, class groups, ethnic divisions, life styles, and sweeping changes in technology and economic organization. Studies of an entire civilization turn to culture full-blown, and examine values and grand class and institutional movements, with individuals assuming bit-parts as the drama sweeps toward twilight. But studies of a crisis must force all or most of these elements into a narrow time-frame, speeding up social time. The velocity of change clearly carries no implications concerning its direction—another way of distinguishing processual from repetitive time concepts. Similarly, the apparent direction of change in a chronological span may not be the same as the general direction in another span, whether longer or shorter.

Thus we can ascribe weights, or differing degrees of importance, to the basic elements of political analysis. This approach is another way of eliminating disputation concerning what is "the" critical element in social change through all time, or other temptations toward monistic explanation. In any situation, the variable (or variables) that "pull" hardest in influencing other action depends on the number of other variables in play and the time period in which they are working. The limiting hypotheses would seem to be:

—The shorter the time span and the fewer the variables, the more likely it is that individual factors will be the most influential in providing a satisfactory explanation.

—The shorter the time span and the larger the number of variables, the more likely it is that equal weight will have to be given class, institutional, and personal factors—and, in extreme cases, even value factors; that is, the more likely it is that social organization will implode, imbuing all social phenomena with equally critical significance.

—The longer the time span, the more likely it is that value systems will have the greatest explanatory power, although these will have to be used in concert with the other analytic elements, with decreasing weight being given to each in the order of its susceptibility to variation. (The suggestion has already been advanced that, in the order of their resistance to change, the elements go from values to class, institutions, and individual factors.)

The last proposition brings us into the realm of such thinkers as Spengler, Marx, Toynbee, and Weber. I will venture only a short distance into this treacherous domain, in order to explore hastily what is on the other side of the limited boundaries set for this book. The sketchy map of that land I carry with me was drawn by Weber. In essence, I accept his argument that, in the very beginning, there is the idea. He sees that idea as assuming social sense through an ethos—a cultural understanding, a world-view, a matrix for framing other, lesser understandings. He takes pains to point out that no one can be free of all-embracing cultural frames, and I assume that part of my own inheritance impels me to question limits of understanding and to push them as far as empirically possible, retaining all the while a value preference that understanding is good in itself. The passion of the desire to know provides the drive which creates the passion to examine that desire. Differentiation is a characteristic not merely of the institutional orders of modern society. There is personal differentiation: the ability to be inside and outside of one's society at the same time; to be engaged citizen and objective scholar in mutual complementarity; to believe that it is an ultimate truth that we can know only relative validity. These dialectics comprise some of the more important syntheses of western culture. I cannot believe they have no relation to the lesser actions that have been my only subject matter so far.

The belief that ideas consecrated as cultural values have a very long-term influence inspires egotistic satisfaction, as do shorter-run indications of man's power to choose. And since ideas are made by men, we return through yet another route to the necessity for accepting a certain responsibility for and satisfaction in what we are, and do, and can do. The particularities of the grand patterns which have evolved remain our major interest, but we could not have known the limits of our specificity without this brief indulgence in what lies beyond.

A Typology of Traditional and Modern Societies

To this point, we have presumed that the more differentiated the institutions of a society become, the more are the synaptic connections among them (and among them and class, normative, and personal factors) subject to consciously determined design. This assumption leads us to add that the less elaborated a society, the weaker its ability to decide its own make-up. The wish to examine the potential for choice naturally drives us to examine structured and differentiated, or what we commonly call modern or developed, societies; but absent from this analysis so far is a statement of comparison that will permit us to distinguish these from more primitively structured societies. We need a typology of societies that will guide us to the kinds of politics we expect each type to be able to carry out. Otherwise, we shall simply be referring to some polities as more autonomous than others, and we shall have no ordered way of judging how much any one system is fulfilling its potential either for reasoned choice or for greater authoritarianism. Our typology should provide guides to categorization that will cover all cases and permit us to order them into clusters of related empirical phenomena. In other words, we should use measures that can provide continua to range all cases on, and others that provide continua only within given categories of cases. Then, if we succeed, we can distinguish change within a category from change describing movement from one category of social event to another. The latter—the movement of societies from one kind of primary organization to another—necessarily involves both value and community conflict; change within a category does not invite such deep-seated trouble. The former is always revolutionary, the latter only sometimes so. The former are always qualitative and involve more than simple agglutinative changes in size or extension; the latter may well be simply quantitative.

Stratification, the degree of institutional diffuseness or differentiation, and appropriate norms will be the standards for division. Stratification, as we have pointed out, is a universal phenomenon whose significance comes from its particular configurations. Institutions—routinized behavior patterns—are always present, too, of course, but for our purposes we must emphasize the degrees of discreteness among them. Norms are also susceptible to the same generality-specificity dichotomy. Grouping all three elements in categories is done in harmony; that is, we cluster the three elements as they would appear if consistency reigned, remembering that in real life inconsistency is the rule. In addition, because our interest lies in more rather than less developed situations, we shall discuss the less structured cases with little detail. Throughout, as the typology describes the movement from tribal to national organization, I presume increasing potential political power. As a simple framework, then, for the following discussions of development and modernization, this is the suggested typology:

1. *Stratification in Institutionally Diffused Cultures with Dominant Organic Value Systems* (stratification only, no classes, by age, sex, occupation, etc.; the criteria of stratification are determined by imputed level of technological development):

Nomadic societies, including sub-groups referring to endogamous and exogamous marriage patterns, etc.

Semi-nomadic societies, with appropriate sub-groups as above.

Settled village cultures, endogamous, tribal.

Settled village cultures, exogamous, non-tribal.

2. *Stratification in Institutionally Differentiated Cultures* (by sex, age, occupation, etc., and by social class):

Closed, non-mobile class systems (ascription societies);

class/caste societies with rigidly defined social distinctions and organic socio-religious value systems.

Partially open, mobile class systems (achievement societies); classical early national three-class societies (with their historical subdivisions) with limited mobility between upper and middle groups, and developing relativistic, pragmatic, and change-recognizing value systems.

Modern multi-class systems with routinized mobility channels during periods of growth (the mobility proceeding along differentiated political, economic, and social channels), highly articulated value systems, and differentiated institutional structures; "the nationally participant society."

The simplicity of this typology will not conceal its ideological and predictive thorns, the principal one being ideological, repeating the earlier bias that there are qualitatively different kinds of humans in the world. For to say that societies differ in their nature strongly implies that one believes there are different types of men inhabiting them. Their dissimilarities are not merely normative, of course, but also behavioral and affective. The cultural gulf such disparateness produces has been expressed as follows:

It is disquietingly true that, as Boas pointed out, "primitive society . . . does not favor individual freedom of thought"—a generality hardly worth making if a *generic* difference had not been felt between the world of *tabu* without formal law and the world that at least wrote, however imperfectly it observes, bills of rights. Or take it this way: For generations the western world has bitterly blamed western man for the crime of not understanding the savage. It seems never to occur to anybody that, other things being equal, it would be equally fair to blame the savage for not understanding western man. Since that would obviously be absurd, the two sets of cultures are unmistakably on different levels, a statement that can be made without specifying higher or lower.[1]

The generic difference pointed out here helps us to understand the vast distance that indeed separates certain kinds of individuals and societies. But certainly it is not absurd to ask "western man" to understand the "savage." One of the most important components in the cultural make-up of western man *should* be precisely an ability to understand the "savage," whether the latter be in an Asian rain forest or living next door in Greenwich. The typology presented here helps us to see that the path of empathy goes from more to less developed—particularly useful knowledge when differing cultures meet on the international scene. It will also help us to determine when differing culture groups live in the same political nation, thereby saving us from the error of presuming a national community where only pre-national communities exist.

We can also imagine a much more complex categorization, in which the elements are inconsistently mixed. It is worth going through a sample exercise to illustrate another way of approaching the asymmetry I have spoken of, and to feel the reality of these classifications. We might, for example, imagine a society with an elaborated class system and a highly differentiated institutional order, but politically dedicated in international affairs to a simplistic and disdainful world-view, seeing other people as venal power-seekers motivated only by greed and envy, and easily moved by

[1] J. C. Furnas, *The Anatomy of Paradise* (New York: William Sloan Associates, 1937), p. 478.

physical fear and material temptation. Such a nation might confront another country with a simple class structure and an early industrial institutional order, led by a charismatic leader motivating his followers by traditional appeals toward modernist behavior—that is, impersonal dedication to nation-building, a willingness to sacrifice today for tomorrow's gains, a practical ability to project through time and space because the leader so wills it, and so forth. The result might be that the physically more powerful nation would act in traditional nonrationality, while the weaker, less developed state would behave in highly effective, pragmatic, and rationalistic ways. Examples of such apparent contradictions are amply available—Soviet Russia versus Yugoslavia, and the United States versus North Vietnam come readily to mind.

The utility of our typology for certain kinds of gross prediction can be shown by yet another example in international affairs already mentioned in passing. In 1954 a small rebel force entered Guatemala from Honduras and handily succeeded in overthrowing the incumbent government led by Colonel Jacobo Arbenz. The invasion force, supplied by the United States, was successful primarily because the Arbenz administration was not backed by a citizenry that could answer his call to arms, or even by a bureaucratic or military structure that would respond to his or anybody else's call to joint political action. In 1954 over half of Guatemala's population of three million was Indian, almost ninety per cent was illiterate, and we may assume that no more than one-tenth could be counted as even potential members of a national community. From this latter group came all the government employees, the military forces, the white-collar and industrial employees, the businessmen and the industrial community, etc. The Guatemala of 1954 was unprepared to fight any kind of "modern" war in the sense of employing a loyal citizens' army. In placing Guatemala in our typology, we would have to divide it between institutionally diffused village cultures on the one hand, and a cross between an ascriptive class society and a very early version of a partial achievement system. That the country will fit in no single categorical box indicates the true cultural pluralism of Guatemala. Because our typology is culture-based, it must be designed to accommodate tri-cultural situations in three different categories, all of them comfortably fitting class and caste divisions. From the point of view of those coping with the practical problems of subverting Guatemala's government, it was quite a convenience that the country had to have a weak central government, an easy prey to determined threat.

The invasion of Cuba at the Bay of Pigs in 1961 was modeled on the Guatemalan episode, although more might was involved. Even so, the invasion force numbered only several thousand men, and they were by no means equipped with the latest weaponry. In Cuba, contrary to the Guatemalan case, the citizens did not desert the government: some remained indifferent, the opposition was passive or quickly rounded up, and military and civil strength was quickly mustered to permit the Castro government to overcome the invasion handily. The invasion attempt failed primarily because Cuba was in the process of becoming a nation-state and thus could count on its citizens to come forward in sufficient numbers to die in defense of the state. We have no way of knowing what would have happened had the combat gone on longer, but there is some probability that Cuba would have witnessed an early version of a modern war involving large numbers of its civilian population. In terms of our typology, Cuba would rank as a partially open and mobile class system, with limited mobility patterns rapidly being expanded by the government and assisted by the flight of refugees leaving open their posts, and with a pragmatic leader employing charismatic appeals to lead a partially willing populace.

The Guatemalan and Cuban cases represent two different kinds of social events taking place in two substantively different countries. The difference was predictable before the fact.

Modernization Distinguished from Development

The conditions that make developmental change possible spread through the entire spectrum of our typology, but the causal possibilities for modernizing changes occur only at specific points of the categories. *Modernizing* social change occurs when the area of rational and effective choice is widened at the same time that the number and types of persons and groups who can participate in making significant public decisions increase. Modernization eventually meshes total populations in impersonal, secular, and empirically rational procedures of a kind that are possible only in elaborately structured situations. *Developmental* change increases the level of specialization and institutional differentiation of a society. Development has to do with the growth of industry, the elaboration of an educational system, the evolution of a national community and its appropriate system of political consensus and legitimacy and authority. The separation of church and state, and the growth of a contractual market economy, including some elements of competitiveness and other earmarks of impersonality, are also usual concomitants of development. Developed societies need not be modern ones. Modern ones must be developed.

The freedom to make rational and effective public choices is the key distinguishing mark of the citizen of a modern polity, a polity that is different from all others precisely because it gives the power to, and maintains a structure of procedures for, all rational citizens to make effective their public preferences in complex and impersonal situations. The test of social modernity is whether significant parts of an institutional structure can be changed without touching off an explosion of irrationality, violence, and destruction, and without other well-functioning organizational relations breaking down. There are no totally modern societies—no societies that can unquestionably and unfailingly continue to make institutional changes that enlarge the area of effective and rational choice.

These statements are definitional, to be sure, their worth being only in their utility. Distinguishing between development and modernization separates the universal from the particular, making useful discriminations for limiting the variety of cases to be put in our categories. If modernization and development are considered synonymous, Nazi Germany and parliamentary England would fall in the same box, for example, and such a category is obviously too gross for any refined political purposes.

The usual indicators of development are a literate populace, an adequate per-capita income, industrialization, urbanization, extensive systems of communication, and elaborated class structures. All of these, however, are compatible with both totalitarian and democratic political forms and thus are not sufficient by themselves to explain grand political organization. They cannot be finely discriminating political criteria because they are not cumulative; that is, they are not additive in the sense that in combination they can describe a conglomerate and yet significant social picture which correlates with a refined range of political situations. Assembling such indicators, then, is merely a starting point, which provides only bald description without inherent power to explain the quality of political life.

So far, we have considered with respect to change only the processes of development—the elaboration and specification of class and institutional and normative orders. Modernization as an expression of rational libertarianism must now be discussed in more detail, if we are to use the two concepts together as an analytical tool instead of a polemical bludgeon.

A "rational" political choice is arrived at through a pragmatic and relativistic consideration of the relevant information on the entire range of possibilities open at the moment of analysis and likely to be open at a proximate future time. It is not rational to propose to do the impossible, or to make a decision without considering the full range of possibilities. The alternatives will, of course, change as the level of social development rises. Thus, a modern ideology must accept, value, and put to use scientific method as a primary procedure, and the institutional order must provide a way to express preferences among possible alternatives. The role of the scientist (social or physical) in policy decision then becomes clear: he is equipped to assist in determining the range of meaningful decisions open at any given time, place, and society. When the time for expressing his preference arises, he should step into the role of a citizen, letting his specialized function cede to his generalized one.

In any situation demanding special expertise, the entire process of arriving at such rational determinations clearly cannot be the work of a single man or a small oligarchy. So many bodies of knowledge are involved in a national decision that no one man or small group of men can have the capacity to act rationally. Above all, a synthesis of the specializations is needed, to focus the knowledge and judgment required for weighing the costs against the benefits of choice. And a free flow of information is imperative, to ensure that the pertinent information is at hand or can be uncovered. Without it, public understanding of the alternatives cannot exist, and the preferences then expressed will not rest on a base of knowledge which justifies the consensual acceptance of a participating and concerned citizenry. If the power created by consensus is not considered in making the choices, their effectiveness is cast into doubt. And that very weakness signifies a failure of rationality, of course, because there has been a limiting of the sphere of effective choice.

Another critical aspect of a rational approach to decision-making is that the proposals passed on to the ideological level for choice based on political taste should indicate which avenues lead to an area of decreased rational choice, and which to enlarged possibilities for future choices. In both science and politics, self-defeat lies in unnecessarily trammeling the future by the present. If we find desirable the use of rationality as instrumentality, then it would be pointless—or irrational—to turn it on itself.

I have already advanced the idea that ineffective choices are neither socially relevant nor rational. Ineffectiveness may stem from the technical inability of society to accomplish given purposes, or from the political weakness of the persons and groups making choices. Effectiveness is not to be ascertained by determining whether the given choice becomes public policy. Rather, the criterion is whether the expression of preference becomes part of the general political process of making decisions. Whether we have the freedom to make and express an effective choice is in part judged by whether it is taken as part of the basis for broader choice-making, a component both of the rational consideration of possible choices and of the political applicability of choice. In these two senses the citizen's effectiveness is essential in establishing the effectiveness of proposed policy.

Exclusions from the area of effectiveness are in the first instance usually along class and racial lines. These exclusions are rationally justified only when full societal liberty and power are not accepted as national goals by those in control. The search for complete development, however, is blocked when there is ostracism of social groups and a denial of public freedom. The heightened efficiency that accompanies development depends in large measure on the efficacious recruitment of the people who are most competent to perform specialized tasks. Limiting the base of participating society obviously impedes rational personnel selection; it limits the size of the effective consuming public, too, and decreases the society's potential for savings and investments. Denying people admission to national institutions, or expelling them, also reduces the power of the state by limiting the consensual acceptance of its dicta and by increasing the need for police power to impose the law on citizens who have not been given the chance to endorse it.

If, then, the goal of the rulers is to maximize their relative economic power and to hold a monopoly of political power within an only partial national community, then it is rational, in a limited sense, to have two different kinds of persons in the same political system. Aristocrats may find a traditional system highly desirable—for the cheap labor that provides an abundance of personal service, and for the comfortable certainty that the deference, political power, and economic control accorded them can continue hand in hand. They will see development as desirable because it brings greater purchasing power for industrial products as well as personal services, and it puts a high order of technology at their disposal to keep subordinate groups in their places. The rewards are, indeed, pleasant. It is nice to have automobiles and peons to wash them after every use. Washing machines are splendid, but they are even better with a laundrywoman to operate them. Large families are less of a trial when television sets can alternate with nannies in the care of children.

The relatively easy transfer of technology is a recent ability. Thus, mixed regimes of the kind I have been discussing have matured only recently, and we do not know much about their survival power. It can be guessed, however, that the core problem of such elite systems, with their middle-class allies, lies in the ever-present possibility of failure in their ability to control the elements of repression needed to keep the system functioning. As world ideology changes and as domestic conditions mature, it is probable that the maintenance of an alienated and non-participant lower group will depend on moving from traditional to totalitarian control mechanisms. And aside from the vertical class tensions that occur when the screws of repression are tightened, there would probably also be intra-class discord within the leading groups themselves. As the softer authoritarianism of tradition cedes to the more rigorous practices of developed totalitarianism, the comforts of the elite can become so many trials. Nevertheless, recent history in Greece, Spain, Portugal, and many Latin American states suggests that mixed systems can persist for many generations, and that one cannot dismantle them rapidly without violence.

Another kind of exclusion from political effectiveness stems from the belief-systems of individuals who choose not to participate. Voluntary alienation is expressed by some university students, to give just one example. The reasons for student discontent of this kind are obvious enough: the problem is not class or occupational exclusion, but the feeling that their views, desires, commitments, and very lives are not positive elements in the making of their nation's political decisions. Trite as this illustration has become, it does cast light on an important sense of the meaning of effectiveness, and it suggests that ineffectiveness stemming from community definition is different from ineffectiveness due to ideational disagreement. The widespread feelings of uselessness in American politics today also indicate a certain independence of structural from normative interests. Many black leaders dissociate themselves from college youth, for example, arguing that white dissidents can go home whenever they wish, while the Negro is forced to live his dissent—that is, that the black problem is structural, the white one "artificial."

Ideological disagreement necessarily concerns the *quality* of the disputed situation, whether the view is that institutions should be destroyed or amended. Groups excluded for class or race reasons may press to change the power structure, but they also may be merely quantitative in their desires, pleading only for entrance into the system. Qualitative dissent may or may not be modernizing in the sense the term is used here, but quantitative disagreement alone is in its very nature only developmental and thus cannot be consciously modernizing. An exclusionist society can increase the number of its participants without changing the attitudes and the reasons that led to the exclusion in the first place. The newly incorporated groups often subsequently adopt the same bigotry that beset them, applying those values to other parts of the internal proletariat or outward in the pyrotechnics of xenophobia.

The Grand Politics of Partial Democracies

In Chapter II, I allowed "libertarianism," "freedom," "rationality," and "pragmatism" to flow together in meaning. I also began cautiously to use the word "democracy," despite having noted in the preface the charges that "democracy" in certain places and times is considered but a cover for imperialism and other forms of repression. And at times democratic states have certainly been guilty as charged. Still, despite the many and continuing outrages committed in the name of democracy, the democratic orders of this world are much more than circuses of the hypocritical.

Although democracies have violated their stated ideals inside and outside their borders, some of the groups within their societies have enjoyed advantages that are normally and accurately called democratic. Other groups have not. Reasonable equality before the law has protected only fully participant citizens; for them alone, religious freedom has been observed; schools have helped some students to personal growth; ideologies of social decency have been forged and partially applied; and the rights of certain minorities have come to be respected. Irish immigrants to the United

States have grown up in a more rather than less democratic society. Southern sharecroppers have grown up in a less rather than more democractic society. The black population has lived in an authoritarian subjugation to the rest. In truth, the partially free and the partially enslaved have managed to coexist for a long time in all democratic states. Perhaps Lincoln will be proved right in the long run, but many have starved intellectually, spiritually, and physically waiting for his aphorism to come true.

Like other societies, then, democratic ones can arrest their modernization. They do so when they surrender to class and color definitions of "ins" and "outs" and obey precepts that oppose the standard democratic credo of equality before the system and its laws. Marxists argue that this is unavoidable, a historical necessity inherent in any society that maintains the fact of class. The formalistic democrat proclaims the system to be good and asserts its ability to accept new recruits as soon as they prove themselves ready for admission. The radical democrat should maintain that the system must work actively to spread its coverage, that the system can succeed because human will and organization can overcome "fatal" historical "necessities," and because to wait for the exploited to free themselves is unjust, inefficient, and an open invitation to irrational responses from all sides. To stall the process of democratic change invites the live possibility that partial democracies will become more authoritarian, or perhaps totalitarian, for only anti-democratic measures can prevent democracy's extension. Treading water is only a temporary alternative.

Unlike other societies that maintain multiple systems of belonging and non-belonging, the democratic society has some portion of the mechanisms, values, and ideologies required for a libertarian politics of reason in a fully participant community. It has been sufficient to permit middle and upper strata to exercise a degree of effective and rational control in promoting the material development that is evident wherever there is some ration of democratic organization. In addition, all democracies possess the stock of ideas that can promote their continued development. That the same optimistic conclusion cannot be drawn so all-inclusively for non-democratic ruling groups is another way of underscoring the qualitative differences between imperfect democracies and the many forms of authoritarianism.

Class and the Structure of Democratic Institutions

The genius of the democratic order is that it has found a way to mitigate the anti-developmental effects of class division. Its sickness appears when its genius is betrayed, when the institutionalized rationalism of a freely consenting populace is sacrificed to the statics of privilege maintenance. Authoritarianism can promote economic development, of course. But only freely rational organization can *continue* development without breakdown.

Let the reader be shocked with a statement seeming to reek of ethnocentrism: all those countries usually counted as among the world's most developed nations are Protestant, capitalistic, nationalistic, and democratic. Let me hastily add that I know the Japanese are not Protestant and that the Russians are neither Protestant nor capitalist. I could have blunted the pain of my assertion by restricting it to countries recognized as being developed for fifty years or more. But this caution would not reflect what I am trying to say—that there is something in the essence of social organization

implied by Protestantism, capitalism, nationalism, and democracy characterizing all states that have succeeded in creating a reasonably balanced institutional approach to full
development. Those massive idea-systems all describe a relationship between individuals and their total societies that
mitigates the effects of the class order.

In elaborating this statement, I shall do violence to some
classic social theories by taking them out of their historical
context in order to single out what I think is their modernizing and developmental essence. For our purposes, the
principal lasting modernizing effect of the sixteenth- and
seventeenth-century natural-law theorists was their limitation of the social impact of religious belief. By arguing that
all men are equal before the natural law, and that all institutions are to be submitted equally to the same criteria
concerning their conformity to this law, they postulated
equally applicable sets of measures to man and his social
doings. To hold that natural law is the same for all is not
to argue that all men are empirically equal before that natural law, but at least it opens the door for thinking that all
men are touched with grace, and so takes a step toward removing religion as a measure of worth determining a man's
secular position. In addition, these theorists established a
basis for reconciling individual with social good by propos-
ing identical criteria for the ethical judgment of each. The
basis for a totally secular approach to politics was laid earlier
by Machiavelli. In this sense, he was ahead of his time. The
reinfusion of natural-law doctrine into political thought by
English and French theorists was done in such a way as to
permit dual secular and religious structures that shared an
explicitly stated set of ethical principles. This theoretical innovation permitted man to be both religious and secular,

an updating of Old Testament thought not unnoticed by the philosophers of the period.

It may be objected that England has an official, established church and that many Protestants are extraordinarily bigoted in religious and racial affairs. Of course. The establishment or disestablishment of a church does not in itself signify whether church and state are separated for practical public purposes. In some Catholic countries establishment often signifies that the church is under state control in matters including even nominations for the appointment of bishops. That many Protestants are bigots is undeniable, as the Bible belt attests. But we are, of course, using Protestantism in the Weberian sense of an ethic, or ethos. The broad culture-area called Protestant devised a world-view which, among other things, permitted the idea that all men are equal before the natural law, and therefore that no man should be judged as citizen according to his creed or religious belief. It is not that all Protestants or all Protestant lands show an unbroken record of adherence to this idea, but merely that its existence and partial operation eventually permitted many persons to become available for membership in the national community who otherwise would have been barred.

The growth of early capitalist thought was coherent with these natural-law views on religion, and not only because the automatic workings of a competitive market mechanism were thought to conform to natural prescription, or because the Doctrine of the Invisible Hand was an aesthetically pleasing statement of the consonance between private and public welfare. The human basis of economic endeavor had already been set forth by Locke's labor theory of value. From the assumption that value is entirely man-produced, it was but a short step to advocating an impersonal market economy, one based not on individuals as status-inheritors, but on individuals as value-creators. Theological views on interest and the use of capital, as well as ascriptive judgments concerning individuals, were ideally to be put aside in the market itself. The ticket of admission for the consumer was money—not skin color, accent, or ideology. The ticket of admission for the producer was money or skill. Accumulating profits into huge lumps large enough to achieve monopoly would be discouraged by competition and the erosive effects of time. The presumption was that multiple producers competing against one another as well as against consumers would lead to a total price of goods on the market equal to total cost. Although at given moments individual producers would make profits while others would lose, the competitive drive would cause unprofitable procedures either to find more efficient means of production, or else go bankrupt and leave room for more effective innovators. For Adam Smith, the monopolist was the most despicable of men.

Nevertheless, it is doubtful that competition is the key to capitalist efficiency. Although the supposition is not easily proved, the partial broadening of recruitment to economic activity probably was and is a much more significant factor. So, too, are the secularization and expansion of consumer publics, and the rationalizing sense that took hold of the entire economic enterprise. The increasing productivity of the American economy can only marginally be explained as the result of competitive urges, learned or innate. The desire to make money can usually be satisfied in ways involving none of the disagreeable uncertainties of competition.

As Berle and Means, Polanyi, and Sherman testify, a truly competitive, free, universally open market economy has never existed. One of the fallacies of advocates of a free market economy is that man can think in "pure" economic terms and then act on what he thinks. I have taken some pains to argue that the connection between beliefs and behavior is not necessarily coherent. Departures from the norm with respect to competitive freedom and even the desire for monetary gain occur constantly. In the name of free enterprise and profit-taking, Southern pharmacists have refused to sell coffee to Negroes. Trade unionists often subsume economic to political motives. But even though the self-correcting market mechanism has never operated fully in accord with its theoretical design, the belief in an impersonal market mechanism has contributed to development wherever it has been seriously translated into some measure of practice.

Equality of opportunity in the marketplace is most difficult to achieve in the face of the facts of class. Inherited and corporatively accumulated wealth transmit market advantages through time, and inheritance laws have not hindered this pattern. The technological desirability of economies of scale has become far more important than the public-utility monopoly or the classical "trusts" as a cause of combination and monopoly. Seen in this light, the development of socialist ideology was a response to the inherent inability of the market economy to remain as competitive as expected by the original theorists of a capitalist order, who foresaw some but not all of the political-economic reasons for accumulations of power in the market. Socialism ties economic power to class power, and both to the imposition of arbitrary political control as a means to maintain class privilege. Whatever the elaboration of the doctrine beyond this point, the time perspective we occupy should indicate that over-all, socialist ideologies share important premises with the classical ideologies of democratic capitalism. Both are fearful of overconcentrations of economic power, both favor equality, and both look for devices to prevent economic power from controlling other institutions to the detriment of a pluralist safeguard against autocracy.

If capitalist theory has little to suggest on how to maintain equality of competitive chances among those injecting capital into the market, it does offer a method of equalizing skills, the major personal productive element. A high-quality and complete public-school system is in every state a crucial step in mitigating the effect of the accident of birth on the performance of economic roles. Opposition to public education was initially bitter, and public education is still an unfinished task even in the United States and Great Britain. Opposition to taxes, misplaced political priorities, and inattention have contributed to a continuing decay of public education in the United States. The decline in quality of many grammar and high schools in American cities also underscores how a racial conflict concerning the extension of community affects institutions. As the race-conscious Southern pharmacist sacrifices economic to racial interests, and thus goes backward in social development to primitive wholeness, so does the weakening of a public-school system threaten to retard the rate of economic growth.

Secular public education not only provides manpower for the economy, but it also slowly contributes to the creation of a new kind of competitiveness. The contemporary democratic approach to control of economic power has been not through the economic institution alone, but has involved political and social elements. Collective bargaining, consumer awareness, knowledge of market conditions, the proliferation of pressure groups, boycotts and strikes and other demonstrations, are all ways of influencing economic decisions. They involve the primary political act of organization, an act which in significant measure is a product of education and the learning of alternatives that accompanies it. For example, price-setting is viewed more and more as only one among many ways that power is applied. The notion that general social power can affect prices, and thus patterns of distribution, is as "natural" as the classical economic view of the "naturalness" of economic man in his sealed marketplace. To see the economic structure as one of many arenas of power contention is also to see it as susceptible to beneficent rational control, and not as an automatic and thus a-rational pattern of activities.

Theorists of capitalism have been clearly empirically wrong in their belief that automatically self-correcting market mechanisms were operating. They were clearly developmentally right in seeking a system that would equalize the conditions under which man would have access to his economy. The practice of such equality demands a liberation impossible so long as family, religion, and race remain determinants of personal worth, matters that today's economists rarely worry about in any systematic way.

Nationalism as a statement of the relation of the political institution to social community is another method of permitting individuals to assume their own and confront others' social roles free of the chains of ascription. Equality before the laws and the agents thereof is what the completely national state owes to those within its jurisdiction; loyalty to the legitimately acting community and its lawfully circumscribed public servants is the citizens' correlative obligation. In developing lands, nationalism is invariably equated with freedom from foreign yokes and with the creation of a sense of nationhood; it is revolutionary in that it seeks to bring previously alienated groups into the national community. In developed lands, nationalism tends to take on a negative connotation—xenophobic, an excuse for the continued exclusion of pariahs, anti-internationalist, a cause of war. Both interpretations have their reason for being. In the former case nationalism is needed to create the power required to stay the hands of foreign interventors and to develop resources, power that can be generated only by including new masses within a system of national identification and interaction.

Nationalism in the United States has been seriously misunderstood because of ideological confusion. Many Americans who denounce nationalism have a profound respect for the worth of a system dedicated to a continuing and instrumentally open-ended search for individual betterment. Despite their denial of being nationalistic, their ultimate loyalty to a democratic America gives predictability to law and strength to nation. Their acceptance of a just and equitable state as the ultimate, impartial arbiter of secular dispute is a commitment as firm as their concomitant belief in a political system under which they can change laws they believe to be undesirable or unjust. They accept the state in its classical liberal sense, as an artifact. This profound loyalty to a secular system is evinced even by dissidents who break specific laws in order to arouse support for their repeal. Such loyalty is rarely xenophobic, however, for those who demonstrate it also tend to identify with persons outside their own political community. Their internationalism, then, is an expansion of national community, through which a dedication to their own culture group is extended outward to embrace others. No inconsistency divides these perceptions of nationhood as actuality and as a society open to wider identifications.

Many people who call themselves nationalists in the United States would keep membership in the nation within narrow ethnic or ideological limits. They think a nation-state, like a country club, can function with a carefully controlled membership. But to equate nation with specific class strata or given "races" denies the idea of total national community and inhibits the full realization of its positive developmental potential. Such nationalists are dangerous precisely to what they profess to support. Unhappily, their beliefs give them some of the strength that comes with far-flung and yet tightly interdependent and predictable national communities. Thus they can sometimes gather the power to make life hell for those they dislike. Only a partially national society can muster the power to be truly totalitarian. When enough people believe in such a quasi-national society, then all institutional protections can be swept away from the individual, who is left naked before the power of a state armed with the weaponry of advanced science and manned with the persons who know how to make it work.

Semi-developed, traditional, non-national authoritarianism is a different kind of system. Its prime purpose is to prevent a national state from seizing a monopoly of public power, leaving church, economic order, and other sectors bereft of their oligarchical strength. Those other influence centers give people institutional nooks and crannies in which to hide. The state cannot become too efficient, or it will defeat its traditionalist purpose for being. Franco and Salazar are not junior versions of Hitler, as the survival rate of their enemies demonstrates. Iberian falangism is hardly defensible, but it is worth pointing out that the tired tyranny of Franco Spain has no Siberia, no Maidanek, Dachau, or Auschwitz.

As the strongest form of social organization, national community throbs with threat and promise. Even in its most sublime manifestation, when it assures all members of the community equality before the law, nationalism carries the danger of destructiveness. The victory of liberalism in Latin America, for example, brought with it constitutions and lawyers and legal codes dedicated to the principle of equality. One result was that an illiterate Indian was considered legally equal to a trained Spaniard, a false equality that often caused him to be despoiled of his land in the courts of law. The final massive extension of the hacienda system in Latin America was a product of this kind of equality. The argument that disadvantaged people in the United States should set about "making it" just as all other "arrived" Americans have done comes out of the same misguided definition of equality. A community affirms that its participants have substantive equality before the law by recognizing group and individual differences and establishing reasonable legal classes so as to equalize opportunity and bring about true social equality. Minors, women, and the mentally unfit are given special treatment without much complaint any more. This notion is as old as legal justice. The nation-state, when working toward the integration of the community, establishes *legal* classes in order to break down the effects of *social* classes. Much of the present political turmoil in the United States turns on a conflict between the uses of social class to restrict the nation, and the uses of legal classes to enlarge it. That social-class integrity is being protected in the name of nationalism is a bitter irony from an ideological point of view, but an important reminder that the nation, as a developmental device, makes libertarianism possible but also threatens it. To hark back to an earlier point, the concrete fact of nation is being made into many differing social facts by the actors within the nation.

A formally democratic order is another primary equalizing mechanism; it is of special importance because it gives tone, and direction to the others. A narrow definition of a democratic order will serve our purpose here, and remain faithful to some of the distinctions we have made. Democracy is a system in which the periodic intervention of the electorate in the basic policy decisions and stance of a state is guaranteed. This definition presumes that the electorate will have free access to the polls, that significantly different choices will be offered it, and that the political mechanism will in general terms respond to its expressed wishes. We should also assume that voters will not be asked to decide technical questions concerning which they are not expert, but that they will address themselves to matters that fall within a legitimate clash of interests and of ideology.

This definition is minimal, conservative, perhaps even reactionary. Like nations, the workings of democracy can be restricted to fewer than all the occupants of a political territory, as we have pointed out. Voters may not have the information or the ability to make reasoned decisions, although they must have voting effectiveness if the system is a real one. In addition, they may lack the institutional channels through which the full array of issues and possibilities can be explained to them and through which they can work in making choices. Democracies, in fine, may not necessarily be libertarian, either for excluded groups or for participating members. As democratic systems grow, their appeals are inevitably libertarian, they are supported by libertarian ideology, and they tend to be libertarian for their still limited membership; but as they consolidate, they tend to reflect the newly created vested interests of the development accompanying democracy, and the old tension between the conservative and the innovative sets in. The formal structure of democracy can then become a framework for organizing consensus and legitimacy to stabilize the vested interests, instead of being a machinery for making ever broader rational and effective choice.

A formal democratic structure in a partial national community is an authoritarian device from the point of view of those who abide by its dicta without the opportunity to shape or change them. This point bears repeating here, particularly because democracy is a concept abused by both its protagonists and antagonists. By definition, the underprivileged in any society will live in some type of authoritarian submission to their rulers. When superordinate groups exercise the strength that is theirs in an incompletely modern system, they can do so in pervasive repression or in enlightened reform. Or, they can be secure enough in their strength to adopt a *laissez-faire* attitude toward the troubles of others. A democratic order possesses all the normative, ideological, and organizational clues to libertarianism, but they may be partly or wholly ignored.

Whenever a test is posed to the essential mechanism of democracy (its ability to assure all members of the community equality in political decision-making), the system trembles. If it is decided to continue a politics of exclusion, the members of the democratic nation must use measures that risk either damaging or destroying the system they pretend to defend. If new elements are admitted to the nation—and they are usually from lower social strata—then know-nothing populism and demagoguery become attractive to aspiring leaders. The rational procedure would be actively to promote the continuing creation of a truly democratic national community, thus anticipating pressures for enlargement; this planned change can readily be accompanied by educational and economic reinforcements, which mitigate the dangers of an influx of persons unequipped to handle the complexities and responsibilities of a freedom-seeking democracy. But I have already made the point that not all democracies are libertarian, although libertarian procedures are necessarily democratic.

Whatever its shortcomings in practice, the core of democratic theory is political equalitarianism, the corollary of the equalitarianism promised by the market economy, the divorce between theology and social ethics, and the national community. The ideal tickets of admission to these theaters of equality are, respectively, citizenship, money or skill, the act of being born, and presence within a political jurisdiction—but never social class. At least in theory, advantages or disadvantages accompanying the accident of birth are to be put aside for public purposes.

The Japanese and Russians have their functional equivalents of these elements. Where development has been twisted because certain elements are missing, such as the right of political dissent in the Soviet Union, pressure for their attainment exists and is increasing. But no unchanging principle of conduct decrees that the partial achievement of the power flowing from these leveling devices cannot be diverted to the ends of destruction and repression. If a person's talents are freed by means of equalitarian techniques and then turned to totalitarian ends, Armageddon is invited. If societies are to continue to develop human beings, and not simply machinery and cities, equality needs liberty.

Values and Social Form

Earlier in this chapter, the opportunity to attempt long-term analysis was shunned. The reason was not any skittishness about the millennium as a calendar manifestation, but rather wariness of the temptation to explain everything as a function of ultimate values, to the detriment of the greater analytical power gained by mixing variables in the explanation even of large sweeps of history. Still, it would be intellectual cowardice not to attempt to study values as an influence in cultural style. I shall attempt to construct counterposing cases of the relation between values and institutional form in the hope of being as precise as possible in a short account that attempts to cover so many happenings. If a discussion of organizing cultural value systems must always be amorphous, one can at least hope that descriptions of institutional organization can be more pointed.

I have spoken of equalitarianism as linked to religious, economic, political, and educational forms as they have grown in modern societies. The Protestant and Catholic culture worlds are an obvious pair for testing social practice and value differences, and equally obviously, the emphasis should be on the relation between institutional differentiation and social class in each culture. Both have highly developed institutions; in that sense, both are pluralist. But the idealized uses of pluralism are different. While social practices are not nearly so unlike as the ostensible ideologies of their ruling groups and leading social theorists, there are still notable empirical differences. The Catholic Latin world economically less developed; no Latin country (with the possible exception of Cuba) is a true nation-state in the social community sense; and the practice even of pejoratively titled "bourgeois" democracy has been limited.

Nor does the very word "pluralism" have the same cultural meaning in both. In the United States, for example, pluralism commonly refers to multiple interest and party groups, a distribution of authority among levels of government, checks and balances between them, and other means by which areas of legitimate authority are divided up. In Latin cultures the word has little currency but, when used, usually refers to a distribution of authority within a single, hierarchical structure, the source of the power being at the apex of the power pyramid. The presumption, then, is that all power is delegated downward from the top and can be withdrawn at will; the American presumption is of a relative autonomy of many power-generating and power-applying centers.

Everyday definitions such as the foregoing are helpful in describing the internal workings of established systems, but they neglect the original basis for each system, and they do not fully explain what it is that maintains micro-happenings —that is, what values are held in common so that millions of citizens in Latin America, say, automatically accept (and thereby validate) one kind of pluralism and North Americans another kind. Let us turn first to the Protestant way of relating institutions to class through merit selection, and then consider the Catholic way of creating order and symmetry among institutions and class position.

Institutions that break individuals away from ascription can be justified only by values that favor a hierarchy based on merit. This may seem obvious, but the implications are not. The classical liberal arguments for a merit hierarchy

reject any notion that the state and society may conta.
within themselves some identification with godhead. If true
hierarchy expresses individual competence, then Thomism,
Hegelianism, and the like must be discarded; no ladders of
human community can blur into the other-worldly, and only
individual man can lay claim to a grain of divinity. The argument is that there is only private interest, and that public
mechanisms are justified only insofar as they satisfy private
needs and wants. This belief is a useful antidote to mystical
authoritarian appeals, but may serve unnecessarily to weaken
the liberal case itself, as we shall see later.

Merit is a personal quality and a relative measure when
used as the basis for hierarchy. The determination of merit
must be on a worldly and rationalistic basis, and the areas of
merit are not universal, but contained within one or several
of the institutions containing hierarchy. Individual equality
before each institution is the first condition defining each set
of institutional participants, while the order of influence inside each cluster of activities reflects particular ability and
confers particular power. A long-term merit system cannot be
imagined except within a pluralist order governed by rational
criteria of institutionally limited power. Acceptance of change
and desire to control the future also accompany the idea of
merit; membership in hierarchy must be transitory if intergenerational influences are to be divorced from the transmission of authority through time.

Many contemporary advocates of merit systems neglect the
systemic conditions for their maintenance, and seem to ad-
vocate little more than a circulating elite of technocratic oli-
garchs. The more notorious of the "meritocrats" propose a
system of hard-working managers and engineers, selected for
their abilities and managing a system in which everyone else

is "functionally useless." This view assumes that only system-maintaining functions are "useful," an attitude that implies something about the divisibility of the private from the public interest, about which we shall have more to say later in this chapter. Even on their own grounds, however, our latter-day technocrats do not explain how the continuous selection of the most "meritorious" from an entire population will work. In creating a universal recruitment pool (a necessary pre-condition for rational and efficient selection), how do they propose to neutralize the effects of class, ethnic distinction, values, ownership patterns, distributional patterns, urban-rural difference, variations in education, and so forth? True equality in recruitment would demand a thoroughgoing social revolution—a precondition the meritocrats reject. If merit selection were to continue to be inhibited by social differences, we would have inefficiency and inequality in the mechanisms of choice, and a probably increasing need to apply force to keep the "functionally useless" in their proletarian places. Like pluralism narrowly conceived, the concept of merit selection, when too closely defined, neglects the normative and institutional necessities for its support and the far-reaching implications of what is required to make it functionally continuous.

The classical ideas of the good and the mechanisms for realizing them—as distinct from modern technocratic ideas justified in the public and only secondarily in the private interest—remain an essential part of the Protestant western tradition. They inform great bodies of law, much polemical writing, and the patriotic wisdom passed on through our schools; they also provide the ideological stock of protest as claimant groups press their desires to belong. This ethos and its appropriate behavior are not unalloyed, of course. Counter-currents eddy through western societies, sometimes driving them to anti-developmental, guilt-ridden oppression and other signs of confusion. Individual and social interests are not in clear and self-evident alignment, and the western tradition even questions the idea of social good *per se*. Nevertheless, over the five centuries during which the modern estate has been developing, the long-range trends are more favorable than not to libertarianism. Imperialism, racism, atrocities in warfare, internal and external exploitation, and grotesque perversions of reality have occurred everywhere. But, on the other side, protests against these perversions are widespread, science as a search for validity is well established, rapid communications have laid the basis for world community, the social order has become differentiated and accessible to more persons and groups than ever before, and creature comforts have given a new dignity to body and possibly to mind. If we have been using the power that flows from our social inventions for self-limitation in certain areas, we have been using them for our further liberation in others.

When we turn to the contrasting case, the Catholic Mediterranean universe, we find a bewildering mix of the ideas and practices of all of Europe. The people of this world have, more often than not, chosen institutional patterns which, though plural in terms of number, remain class-bound in hierarchy. Mediterranean pluralism is a mechanism not for fostering equality but for preserving inequality, and it remains subsumed to the facts of social class.

The Doctrine of the Two Swords holds that institutions are socially primary, defining the just position of the individual. Sanctions are either political or religious, with the latter having primacy because the city of man is but prelude to the City of God. Since industrial cities cannot be built on a simple bi-institutional structure, the Spanish response, for example, to the desire for development has been multi-corporate, with the building of many pillars of specialized institutions, each of them striated by class, and recruitment to these striations is a function of the recruit's social position. These "pillars of society," as they were called even in the Renaissance, are the state, the church, industry, commerce, the military forces, agriculture, and, most recently, trade unions. Tie them together and they are the sticks in the emblem of falangism; put an axhead in their center (reflecting the pretensions of the political pillar to supremacy among its institutional fellows), and they are the symbol of fascism.

Corporativism was revived in the late nineteenth century as Catholic Europe's response to the outrages of early capitalist development. The movement was reinforced by the Church itself, which saw dangers in the secularism accompanying the separation of church and state in Protestant Europe. Austria in the 1930s, Fascist Italy, Spain under Primo de Rivera and Franco, and Portugal under Salazar adopted corporate ideologies. Political practice varied, but in at least two critical areas true corporate organization reigned. Trade-union movements in these countries were stifled by state acts that imprisoned the unions in a structure inhibiting their independent organization and bargaining; and, at the other end of the scale, all these countries were or are still governed by oligarchies representing the leaders of each falange. In none of them were the facts of class mitigated, or were any attempts made to permit individuals to have different statuses in different institutional roles. In fact, the very thought that differing statuses could exist in one individual brings shudders to many people of that culture, for they regard such unevenness as the basic cause of the cold loneliness and personal distress which they believe is pervasive in the capitalistic, Protestant world.

Occupation is the prime organizing criterion for corporativism, for it is used as a symbol for class position; that is, low occupational status automatically means low prestige and political power, little if any chance for education, and the other stylistic characteristics (accent, dress, food habits, times of rising and sleeping) that the society accepts as appropriate to the lower classes. Political representation by occupational group is a common device proposed and sometimes partially employed in Mediterranean cultures.

Corporativism, however, is not confined to the Mediterranean world and its extensions. The National Industrial Recovery Act of New Deal days was corporate in inspiration. And the growth of giant industry has encouraged individuals to think of themselves, their families, and their associates in terms of their occupational roles, and to persistently confuse the interests of their companies with those of their commonwealth. Science-fiction writers have long extrapolated such trends into fantasies concerning total systems ruled by corporate enterprise, the *reductio ad nauseam,* so to speak, of the totality of social meaning as response to a single hierarchical fact of life.

The ultimate corporate ethic proposes that the public interest is primary, for it is society that is divine and not man. The folk version of that ethic is narrower, for there the belief is that the family is divine and that society is but an extended family. The ultimate liberal ethic is the view that the private interest is primary, for it is man that is divine and not society. The folk version of that ethic is narrower, for there the belief is that material satisfaction is divine, and that man is but a thermostat to measure the ups and downs of physiological pains and pleasures.

Concluding Remarks

How tempted the deity must sometimes be to paste back together what was torn asunder by Reformation and Counter-Reformation, to construct a society in which public and private interests are both recognized as valid in themselves and yet unable to exist apart. The search for their reunion is as old as the Renaissance. The Doctrine of the Invisible Hand is a conscious effort to make the two compatible, arguing that the legitimate pursuit of personal interest automatically creates the common weal. The Mediterranean argument, starting from the other side, claims that a legitimately wrought public interest creates the welfare of the individual part, sometimes defined as family and sometimes as individual.

The Poverty of Liberalism, a recent critique of liberal thought,[2] makes a strong case for the need for a theory of the public interest if we are truly to respect and enjoy life in what we cannot escape, community:

> The rationale for the free society is not, as Mills implausibly urged, that it accumulates a greater store of knowledge or more effectively satisfies men's private interests. The free society is good as an end in itself for *it is itself a social value!* So long as men mislead themselves into attaching merely instrumental value to the dialogue of politics, they will cherish it no more highly than any

[2] Robert Paul Wolff, *The Poverty of Liberalism* (Boston: Beacon Press, 1968). See esp. Ch. 5.

other means to their private ends; . . . [if] men recognize
the value of the dialogue itself, they will defend it against
its constant enemies, and perhaps even sacrifice their private interests for its preservation.[3]

The author holds the argument at the political level this
book has also attempted to maintain—avoiding the ultimate
nature of being and meaning, and instead posing the social
question concerning cultural definitions of understanding.
Even so, I wonder whether the confrontation between individual and social interest can be dissolved in this way, or
even whether that confrontation is as real as I have made it
out to be in framing the counterposition of the value systems
of northern and southern European cultures. We all know, as
a matter of daily working knowledge, that we live in the dialectic of the individual and the collective. Despite this com-
mon-sense knowing, individualistic theories of interest neglect the social approach and vice versa. Neither emphasis
succeeds in reconciling the dialectic, in synthesizing two analytical modes of thought. Seen in this light, the issue of social
analysis is not how one or the other set of interests is defined
in itself, but rather how the reconciliation between what is
defined as social and what as individual is worked out in
each social system.

Aside from that descriptive approach to interests, however,
we would do well to ask ourselves what the ideal approach is
to the adjustment of private and public interests. Here we
may be led to fit a universal imperative with its empirical
manifestations and even with the possibility of an ethical
criterion. Certainly there is little risk in asserting that individual man is a social being. Individuality and sociability are
not definable except in terms of each other. They set each

[3] *Ibid.*, p. 193.

other's limits in meaning, action, and effectiveness. They are the two-backed animal of human creation.

My view is that private and public interests are identical. The study of their contradictory manifestations in specific societies is necessarily based on culturally bound definitions that say they are different and possibly opposed. But my own value commitment holds that a private versus public interest clash is necessarily hurtful to the interests of both society and the individual—unimaginable as he is outside of a social setting.

Some historical syntheses of individual and social interests come closer to erasing the difference between them than others, of course. If one holds that the promotion of greater individuality takes place simultaneously with the promotion of greater sociability, and that such a process is desirable, then one must also hold that societies close to such a unification of interests are better than societies distant from it. This statement will outrage cultural relativists and people who think that *any* reconciliation between private and public interest is *per se* desirable. The accommodation of the individual to a primitive society takes place within a very narrow context of individual variability and potential differentiation. The accommodation of the individual to an industrial, totalitarian society is also made at the cost of personal variation and choice in many areas of endeavor. The kind of society spawned by a piratical *laissez-fairism* promotes freedom for some at the cost of the freedom of others. In any event, it is not reconciliation of interests that is desirable: it is the recognition of the *unity* of public and private interest, and the creation of social mechanisms needed to satisfy that singleness of interest, which is the measure of the decent society and decent people.

We have reached the point of having to discuss man in his human nature—as individual, inhabitant of community, and bearer and creator of cultural syntheses. I have tried to present an overview of the social and political process that would not bring us to this point without first going through the outlines of how far we can proceed without it. And, by using the design, I hope to be able to explain events as they have occurred, and also to link the empirical with the normative so that we are all aware of the boundary between them, so that the crossing may not involve a mind-rejecting leap.

An underlying premise of this book has been that it is necessary to add choice or custom to the factors discussed in reaching an understanding of how societies act. It seems inane to go through this long process simply to say that events happen because men make them happen, whether consciously or not. Nevertheless, the intellectually serious and difficult part of the matter is to discover how much of what is made to happen is the result of rationality freshly applied, and how much is of rote response; how much it is possible at given times and places to submit to rational choice, all other things being equal.

The truly silly thing, though, is that despite its obviousness, this statement about the human role in social causality is tacit in most contemporary social thought. We are continually told that technology will make us into this or that, or that the population explosion will result in this or that disaster, or that "they" naturally do what they do because they are where and what they are. History teaches nothing, but men do teach history. Machines do not make industrial civilization; managers, laborers, and clerks make machines, and may or may not make an industrial civilization. Population increase does not make for overcrowding; people make people, and apartment houses, cities, standards of living, patterns of distribution, and communications systems. We excuse ourselves by turning technology, history, populations, communications, and economies into blind forces through the simple device of putting our social eyes out. Sometimes, however, making the obvious significant is the glint in the eye that is the first act of re-creation.

The Human Purpose of
Political Action

On symbols, political sins, and human nature;
and on the obligations of modern man

New thoughts and abilities are appearing under the sun.
Escape from the confines of earth is an example and evidence
of these novelties, a symbol of new techniques for being and
becoming that can be constructed for ourselves wherever we
are. To take another example, the history of social organization has always been written in terms of town and country,
cosmopolitan and provincial, worker and peasant. Now, for
the first time since people pulled themselves together for social warmth in hamlets and villages, we are able to erase the
major vital differences between urban and rural living. City
air made medieval man free, but now national, and even con-
tinental air may make man free—or smother him in the bat-
ting of a technocratic, industrial feudalism.

Now, too, we can rethink the dismal science of economics
and begin to frame economic procedures based on the certainty that some wants can be met to satiety. Theories
of value erected on predications of eternal scarcity can cede
to theories of value built on conceptions of personal gifts and
social enrichment—an economics of material satisfactions designed to serve personal dignity. Computation machinery en-

ables us to turn complex operations into a series of automatic and auto-controlling ones that cheapen and ramify many aspects of communications and production, while we can use the same equipment to increase our understanding of social occurrences. Even the dark arts of weaponry have entered a new universe of effect and meaning. World-destroying hydrogen bombs and their carriers are in a different category from the bow and arrow and the explicitness of their man-to-man effects.

These changes are not a smoothly continuing elaboration of past knowledge and ability. They are system-shattering in scientific and technological senses. Whether they are also to be generative of new social forms and behaviors is another question, which can be answered only as we impregnate those developments with sense. Certainly we shall not free ourselves to use these novelties fully so long as we think of them merely as increasing social control of the physical environment. Instead, they might better be thought of as increasing the potential for rational control of the social environment.

A widespread lament whimpers that social inventiveness has not kept pace with technological advance, that our understanding of the meaning of life and social processes lags listlessly behind the questing heads of the physical scientists and engineers, who are busily producing the delights of the new age. Certainly it is undeniable that social thought is not as coherent as scientific theory and that, unlike physical "laws," one cannot send the ordered findings, ideologies, institutions, and historical experiences of social knowledge from one culture to another with a high degree of surety that these will fit altered circumstances. The laws of "hard" science are posited as immutable; the "laws" of social being are mutable. If social "laws" were not so, then we should never have achieved the science and technology that accompanied the modern world into existence. For the physical and natural sciences are not alien to the institutional settings that give them life; they are not in some strange way "ahead of" or "behind" or even "beside" the societies that nurture them. It is not that science is real and society a myth, but rather the opposite; that is to say, the social realities of certain cultures establish the conditions permitting the institutions, symbols, and practices of scientific endeavor to flourish. The presumptions and methods guiding scientific endeavors are no more or less "social" than any other sets of ideas and procedures, even though they may be subject to rather more internal self-correction than others, and at any given moment deal with closely defined bodies of data.

The erratic social application of scientific production emphasizes the degree to which the scientific enterprise needs to be stripped of its mystery and seen in its human context. The social as well as physical sciences suffer from a dismaying gap between what it is presently reasonable to believe valid and those of their findings that are applied to the solution of problems. As the schedules of New York's commuter lines are not affected by the successes in the space program, so the eating habits of the poor have been little changed by our knowledge that malnutrition is linked to mental retardation; and so our ability to transfer technology has failed to halt an increase in the gap between personal incomes in industrialized and developing countries. Explanations for these failures to live up to the state of our arts usually dignify "hard" science and denigrate "soft" social science; the gap between the production and the consumption of physical scientific knowledge is commonly ascribed to a laggard and rigid social order, while the gap between social-science knowledge and public policy is chalked up to the irrelevance and incompetence of the social sciences. It would be foolish to pretend that social-science findings are as reliable as tested physical scientific findings, but it would also be foolish to allege that the social sciences lack organization or validity, that we are at a total loss in our understanding of social processes, or that scientific thought about society is as hesitant and unreliable in prediction as are the workings of governments. To the contrary, it can be argued that our available stockpile even of ideological thought—as distinct from ordered theorizing—offers guides to action far more fitting to our circumstances than the policy decisions actually being made in most states.

Existing normative and scientific equipment suggests much about the relationship between equality and freedom, and about the institutional orders appropriate for achieving them. We are not incapable of linking equality and freedom to reason and rationalization, and in turn to the processes of development. Neither seer nor computer is needed to tell us that masses of depressed and debased people cannot contribute to general social enrichment in any way comparable to their full potential were they sprung free to become entirely human. These ideas are not bromidic; they explain much of the past historical growth of what we narrowly call industrial society, and their rejection in practice explains much of the malaise that leads us to call our civilization "industrial society" instead of something more appropriate. It is true that our minds have been poisoned by determinisms that make man the dependent variable in society. We think that technological innovation will not be denied, that urbanization produces urbanity, that science is a *deus ex machina*, that economic organization determines all other social relations, that factories manufacture industrial man. Still, some social thinkers know that human beings are in truth the independent variable, and that it is precisely the degree to which their independence can be expressed that is the only solid measure of social and personal growth. They know that, *empirically*, technological innovation is constantly denied its full application, that villagers often live in cities, that science is canalized by politics, that marketplaces are the site of genuine power struggles, and that bricklayers, masons, engineers, and bankers build factories that in turn can be run by slave labor, unionized workers, or white-collar employees obeying magnetic tapes. If social scientists do not always agree on such matters, nevertheless we do have some rigorous and elaborated theories, and blocks of research materials spread somewhat unevenly across areas that are very relevant to present problems.

Like any artifact, the social sciences are defined by the terms of their acceptance and uses, and ultimately by a profound commitment as to what social and individual life is all about. Here, too, we are not without ideas appropriate to an ethic of the unity of private and public interest, to a strategy of continued and simultaneous expansion of multiple membership in large and small communities, and to a tactic of rationally applying ordered knowledge to social change.

Ernst Cassirer and those of his philosophical elaborators such as Susanne Langer have argued that the special ability of human beings is the creation, transmission, understanding, reordering, and re-creation of symbols. This ability makes knowledge cumulative and transferable from generation to generation and across cultures. Humans thus do not have to relive the history of the species in the life of every individual. Instead, they have the potentiality of vicariously experiencing all of human history as they live and add their own uniqueness to it. The prime relationship between Weber and Cassirer resides in their common insistence on the role of the mind in creating social reality—Weber in his insistence on value imputation as creating social out of merely empirical events, Cassirer in his seeing this ability as the synthesis of the biological, cultural, and ethical essences of mankind.

One can accept Cassirer's construction as a tool of analysis. Or, as I do, one can go further and make of it a value commitment. To be human is quintessentially good. The primary defining characteristic of humanness is the ability to symbolize. Symbolizing is an unavoidable human activity, and gains ethical value in how it is used. To create, re-create, transmit, and receive symbols so as to expand the ability to do so is a measure of social and individual good *per se*. To engage in this activity in such a way as to restrict the future power to express humanness is *per se* evil, whether the narrowing of this ability proceeds from individual to social levels, or the reverse. If to be human is good, to be more human is better. The more sensitized a person is to the symbols of others in his own time and place, to the symbols of others in his own time and different cultures, and to the symbols of others across all social time and space, and the more that person can assist others to such a richness of symbolic understanding, the more human he is and, so, the better he is. The human purpose of social organization is to promote humanness in this, its most meaningful sense. A society is better or worse in direct relationship to its ability to promote symbolic creation and effective communication at the levels of ability of each one of its members, without regard to those accidents of birth that impart social station.

This view of the good and the bad, which I have presented in the naïve form in which we all hold such beliefs, undoubtedly influenced the way I have advanced propositions in this book. Material development is not a luxury in my eyes. Respect for others and a longing for genuine equality for everybody before society's institutions are not superficial evidences of good manners and trite ideology. Rather, they are key elements in the inextricably mixed ego-social belief that only through such measures can I, myself, become as fully grown a man as my personal capacities and the cultural arts will permit me. My emphasis on how nationalism and class and racial factors define the size and quality of communities is lent ardor by a personal desire to inhabit many worlds and by a disdain for those who would live in withered universes of the stingy. Still, I have tried to present a way of thinking about social matters in such a way that my own commitments would have little or no effect on the independent judgment of my readers. This effort is not the result of wanting to be stylishly value-free, or an ingenuous attempt to separate the "subjective" from the "objective." On the contrary, it is a consequence of the belief that the style of one way of knowing can fit with styles of other ways of knowing, that one man's set of symbols can be shared by others without having to accept particular relations to a total world-view.

Since the subject matter of this conclusion is somewhat different from that of the rest of the book, it can be treated as separable by anyone who wants to do so, and who is sensitive to the varying validations appropriate to differing kinds of assertions. Here, however, is the appropriate place to weave together method of analysis and personal ethical commitment. One thesis of this work is that the mingling of rite and reason in making decisions must be understood as part of any set of

social events if we are to have a social science. As we did in
the discussion of man as a symbol-making creature, we can
use such a statement as neutral hypothesis, or make it an ethical as well as a scientific premise. In choosing to treat it as
value-laden as well as value-free, I imply that a good social
science can also be a guide to good social action. This suggested double use can be tested retrospectively by infusing
some of the earlier arguments of this book with ethical force:
we can approve procedures for deciding conduct that amplify
and ramify human experience in expanding waves, and reject ways of causing that impoverish and stunt experience in
the spastic jerks of irrationality.

Let us return to the most elemental propositions of this
essay, the building blocks of politics, and see how we might
turn their consideration to helping us judge social sin or
good. In the light, then, of both my partially tested scholarly
views and of my personal commitments, I suggest the following listing of destructive political behavior, in an order of intensity starting with the most profoundly evil of them all.

Lying is the most nefarious political offense. One lies by
imbuing an event with meaning one knows to be false. Un-
truths, especially when robed in political, religious, academic,
or business authority, destroy the possibility of creating common perceptions of political events, and therefore can fracture a political community at all levels of participation. The
creator of the lie first divorces himself from its consumers.
Then, through the passage of time that may reveal the lie,
further fracturing occurs: the liar may come to believe what
he is saying; believers become disenchanted; those who accepted on the faith of authority may continue to believe with
the faith of dogma. Not exempted from this indictment are
lies connected with national security and defense. It is far bet-

ter to keep silent than to present false explanations. The politically despicable nature of public falsity is not saved even by a situation of absolute national emergency—for then, above all times, widespread social cohesion based on demonstrated faith in public institutions and the integrity of leadership is a necessity. A narrow faith in personalistic leadership is a poor substitute for a widespread and impersonal sharing of belief and commitment, obtainable only by reducing the gap between events and the predictions based on understanding them. Indeed, it is the growth of complex attachments to community that has made possible citizens' armies and the new loyalties that have so increased the deaths produced by modern warfare.

No argument is intellectually more craven or potentially more damaging to the consensus system of democracies than that the bureaucrat's decision should be accepted in the absence of corroborative data whose revelation would damage the national security. Since the definition of community is a function of shared perceptions, to separate a community into those "in the know" and those out of it, and into those who believe by faith and those by reason, is to allow primary value differences to fracture overlying social identifications. Credibility gaps, then, should be taken with the utmost seriousness by anyone who values both his personal integrity and the integrity of the society he expects to learn from and strengthen by his loyalty.

Political falsehoods create many social events out of one empirical occurrence, threaten community cohesion by opening up the possibility of value conflicts, and promote charismatic and irrational bureaucracies. Such falsehoods tend to produce erratic politics, and this inhibits the future growth of our ability to create and share symbols, thus impoverishing individuals and societies, betraying their essential human purpose. Let us not confuse a mistaken perception with a lie. Error may or may not flow from incapacity. A lie inevitably involves inefficiency and incompetence, behavior below the limits of capacity, a restriction of the choices made possible by the social situations we find ourselves occupying at any given time. Lying is always figuratively suicidal, homicidal, and genocidal, and sometimes it is literally so.

The second most damaging offense is the exclusion of individuals or groups from membership in all layers of community organization, and from institutions. Lying accomplishes a qualitative exclusion from the power to make rational and effective decisions; class and racial discrimination is a quantitative way of keeping people less human—and thus less political—than their personal gifts make possible. I might add that democratic societies are, by definition, ideologically committed to reduce class and race tensions in social organization and to overlook them in the administration of justice. But democratic polities are also committed by historical practice to maintaining schisms which their ideologies condemn as inequitable, inhuman, and damaging to national strength and development. When pressures to extend membership in the democratic community put ideological beliefs under strain, the emergence of underlying authoritarian tendencies is made easier. Then the true sinfulness of discrimination becomes apparent: the underprivileged assume citizenship unable, by and large, to understand or support the extension of the system of freedom that has worked so long to denigrate them. Having been pressed into less than human status, they are unable easily to come into the fullness of human cultural accomplishment that should have been their heritage from the beginning. The relations between social discrimination and societal weakness, and between social discrimination and personal impoverishment, provide an obvious example of the closeness of the analysis and the ethical opinion argued here.

The third most serious political crime is corruption, the betrayal of institutional integrity—whether by selling out, or by performing below the level of competence permitted by individual capacity and the state of learning or demanded by the tasks themselves. Specialization and institutional differentiation are hallmarks of development; corruption eats into these areas of discrete behavior by submitting the standards and practices of one institutional order to the interests and functions of another. The legislator who sells his vote to an economic pressure group is not only betraying his constituents and the trust of his colleagues, but is threatening the integrity of a political system designed to synthesize differentiations and to prevent economic weapons from becoming political ones. A congressman who votes against making birth-control devices available to those who want to use them on the grounds that his personally held religious views prohibit his support, is employing the political structure for religious ends in contravention of the ancient struggle to achieve separation of church and state. Every downgrading of the level of differentiation below the syntheses already achieved is a retrogressively revolutionary attack on a society's development.

Corruption also threatens to separate formal institutional structures from the control of informal, surrounding ones. In the political sphere, for instance, the dishonesty of public officials makes them reluctant to leave office for fear of the criminal sanctions that their successors might impose on them. This justified concern can help to destroy fragile civilian political forms and to cement governments of force in office. Such cases are legion in Latin America, as well as in many of the new nations of Africa and Asia.

Incompetence for the performance of assumed roles is a more subtle form of corruption—and perhaps even more common—than the more notorious form of role betrayal. Here the issue is not the direct surrender of one institution to another's functions, but rather an attack on the workings of a single institution. Recruitment to institutional positions on the basis of ascription instead of merit is a structural cause of lowered competence found everywhere. Continued promotions of individuals until they achieve their level of incompetence is yet another widespread bureaucratic habit. Arguments *ad hominem* also contribute to the base metal of which so many public decisions are forged. And military men perform diplomatic functions; physicians tell the nation how social security programs should be designed; trade unionists decide that family tradition is an important qualification for becoming a plumber. The legitimate expression of political opinions concerning foreign policy, health programs, and apprenticeship is not at issue, but rather the direct manipulation of institutions to turn opinions into acts in the absence of reasoned formulations of problems, debate, and the exercise of competence with due regard for margins of error and for self-correction. Dice are being cast on nuclear-weapons systems, fall-out, pollution, and other matters affecting human survival, with little assurance that the highest levels of competence have been used, on the best possible data, before the evidence is poured into the forms from which appropriate policies expressing ideological and value preference can be extracted.

Interrupting, or destroying, personal dialogue is the last

outrage against a politics of decency to be mentioned here. Its manifestations are many. When neighbors turn a deaf ear to the cries of a woman being murdered, we have an extreme case of interrupting dialogue in that word's full sense—the empathic communication with another human being that is the essence of our humanity. Less shocking but no less significant examples mark all aspects of our life: clinics that demand proof of financial dependability before treating the patient; physicians who will not lend their assistance at the scene of an accident; professors who will not try to understand the question a student is attempting to frame; clerks who cannot muster the energy to thank a customer—all these contribute to an isolation that threatens to make us faceless, invisible to others, and lacking definition to ourselves. Losing touch with other people arrests the ability to establish a firm personal identity, upon which we depend for the internalized points of reference we use to measure others and the society at large.

Lack of the attitudes, styles, knowledge, and inhibitions of a self-appreciation that respects one's own functions as a human being facilitates the lying, rejection, and corruption which institutionalize moral vacuity. The search for an American black identity, for example, is not necessarily a separatist, anti-national, and aberrational occurrence, but can be a necessary prelude to the delivery into the consciousness of all people of the full pain and emotional wealth of the black experience. We are past the vicarious experience of whites explaining what it is to be black, but we should not forget that those exercises helped to free some blacks for the expression of their own *personae*. The positive stock of symbols now being added to our consciousness comes from blacks not transcending their pasts but integrating and identifying with them, as they create other identifications which permit them to be black and other-than-black at the same time. This way of putting it is but an ideological expression of the discussion earlier in this book about pluralism in its institutional and personal manifestations.

Ripping the affective synapses that link people together condemns us to inhabit cells collected into a penitentiary by the sterile ties of the economic and demographic interdependence we need to keep us alive as animals. Dialogue is the channel through which animalness is converted into humanness—if what is fed through the channel are the goods of honesty, available to all, and kept true in their course. The four apocalyptic sins against a politics of freedom make up a single brute which, when weakened in one of its parts, transfuses energies from the others. One cannot destroy it by an only partial rejection of social evil.

The discomfiting question is now before us: what political action is appropriate to a pursuit of freedom? Homiletic proscriptions spring easily to mind. Thou shalt not tell lies, hate thy neighbors, soldier on the job, or remain silent in the face of outrage. If we all act with integrity, social life will proceed soundly. But how are societies to assure themselves that their governors are civically responsible men? How are the leaders going to be forced to be truthful, legislators to avoid conflicts of interest, judges to see mercy as equity and both as pillars of justice? Who is going to force moving companies to recompense customers for damages, upholsterers not to cover up their sins, sausage-makers to trim the fat, and journalists to keep their attributions straight? No political questions are older, and none in greater need of answer at a time when the power to destroy is absolute and the power to create is opening wholly new sets of choices.

There is no substitute for an ethically aware populace active in keeping moving-man and executive honest. The recipe is classical, of course, but the rigor, the intellectual power and energy with which it must now be prepared reflect modern realities. Citizens need a fresh awareness of the moral basis of a democratic order, its egalitarian fundament, and its promise of accommodating unity and diversity for the simultaneous strengthening of nation, group, and individual. They need to think anew about shibboleths, to get reliable information in understandable form, to learn to demand that their leaders recognize themselves as instruments, not autonomous agents forcing good on others or squeezing the juices of some to maintain the privilege of others. Citizens, too, must learn to insist that public institutions not only respond to opinion, but promote regular and ordered political action.

A standard response will be that these expressions of citizenship are impossible because of the implacable opposition of vested interests. Now, of course, to arrive at a situation of continued, rational participation in any country, including the United States, a goodly amount of shuffling about of persons and institutional power distributions is involved. If interlocking directorates of establishmentarians prevent the expansion of public freedoms, then the most probable alternative for *them*, in the absence of concerted public opposition, is to mount dictatorships of containment of a bureaucratic-technocratic type. The requisite ideologies for such a development are already on the scene. They espouse views of the social world that this entire book has been at some pains to refute as poor social science. Now, let us consider them as social ethic.

Technocratic-bureaucratic authoritarians see leaders as groups-in-themselves, considered in isolation without the "guided" taken into account. Many of them, disenchanted with the proletarian romanticism of naïve Marxism, see the "masses" as dangerously destructive of democratic process because their ignorance renders them simplistic and crude in their world-views—and thus authoritarian. As they do not understand that a leader is conditioned by his followers, they also posit a mechanistically behavioral world in which action is fatally conditioned by social circumstances. Leaders have no choice but to lead, followers have no choice but to follow, criminals have no choice but to commit crimes, and the underprivileged have no choice but to be patronized if their lot is to improve. In an age of expanding scientific knowledge, society will perforce have to adjust to innovation, for there is no choice. Conditions change, and so must society. It is better that central directorates of the initiated should manage that change than that unwashed multitudes should be asked to have a voice in what is entirely beyond their capacities. The new science will produce affluence, which will satisfy the creature needs of the flawed. The scientific-technocratic-industrial kings will establish our social policies, and refresh themselves by recruiting their replacements from among the most meritorious. Plato is alive and well in contemporary America.

This white fascism is a possibility. Its proponents like to picture themselves as benevolent and progressive, sometimes radical, and always "realistic"; they lack the conceptual tools to see that their scheme will certainly demand repression to silence the many persons in all stations of life who do not share their vision of the useful, true, and desirable.

As opposed to this anachronistic, mechanistic heir to the outmoded Positivist vision, this book has sought to establish reasonable grounds for a doctrine of the social process that breaks open the black boxes obscuring the causal gaps left in the reasoning of technological and vulgar economic determinists, and by the many other types of mystifiers currently at large. By concluding that choice—whether habitual or consciously rational—forms part of the nexus tying possibilities to social happenings, a view is opened toward a politics of states that are good for individuals, and individuals who are good· for communities. To escape from the imprisonment of the "inevitability" of social occurrences, one must actually exercise choice, and do so in the rational way that will widen future areas of choice.

The educated and the cultured have a greater ability than the less favored to exchange conscious awareness for routineness in their social actions, and thus they have a greater responsibility to exercise their social capacities. That statement calls an elite into action, of course, an elite of sensitive, integral individuals, whatever their station, who are aware that the making of men is our own doing. Politicians, engineers, scientists, academicians, physicians, industrialists, the upper clergy, and their status peers are not the elite of whom I am speaking (although the chances are high that many of the human elite will bear those job labels). These people have the good fortune of being able to make their humanness politically effective more easily than the institutionally dispossessed, but they suffer the difficulty of needing to maintain and even heighten their own standards of performance while they assist in elevating others; moreover, they must hold their positions against attacks from within their own ranks and from outside oppositions.

Action appropriate to a politics of human enrichment cannot be prescribed in a book of this sort, for fitting behavior depends on the situation concerned. At certain times, especially amid the political crudities of underdeveloped lands, withdrawal from the formally established structure is the only viable alternative, whether or not accompanied by violence. In more complex situations, in crises that have not reached total institutional breakdown, almost all human conduct takes on a political context. A warm and affectionate "good morning" can become not only a touching of personalities, but also an extension of community belonging. Abstention from voting can be a highly significant political act, not an expression of laziness. Whatever the conditions, however, the humanizing of politics will be done by people whose definitions of such actions depart from the current cynicisms.

For example, politics should be seen not as the art of guiding the use of legitimized force, but as the art of promoting and synthesizing difference. Power should shed its meaning related to the imposition of will, and assume the broader meaning of having to do with increasing man's ability to control the consequences of choice. And, choice must mean not merely a static selection among available alternatives, but an act of creation that generates new ranges of possibilities, defining the "now" by uniting an assessment of the past with the creation of the future. A free man does not confine himself to a technocratic politics of the possible. His world is that of the politics of the ever-expanding desirable.

It is theoretically possible for profound and positive social change to come about in the absence of violence and blind coercion. It is practically possible in the near future in probably only a very few countries—those with a high degree of national cohesion, many socially sensitized citizens, and a stock of ideological commitments accepting human freedom as the virtue from which flows the essential means for a self-fulfilling social order. Even there, however, there must be a broad recognition that the practice of freedom is the purpose of freedom, as the end of humanness is reached by being human.